Imperial German Army Motorised Troops 1914-18 Volume 2

Armoured Units, Assault Tanks, and the Weapons of Modern Warfare

---

Jacek Zabielski

Helion & Company Limited
Unit 8 Amherst Business Centre
Budbrooke Road
Warwick
CV34 5WE
England
Tel. 01926 499619
Email: info@helion.co.uk
Website: www.helion.co.uk
X (formerly Twitter): @Helionbooks
Facebook: @HelionBooks
Visit our blog at helionbooks.wordpress.com

Published by Helion & Company 2025
Designed and typeset by Mach 3 Solutions (www.mach3solutions.co.uk)
Cover designed by Paul Hewitt, Battlefield Design (www.battlefield-design.co.uk)

Front cover: An A7V of the 2nd Assault Tank Detachment (*Sturm Pz. Abt. 2*) goes to the front in the spring of 1918. (Photo: Author's collection / AC).

ISBN 978-1-804517-65-9

British Library Cataloguing-in-Publication Data.
A catalogue record for this book is available from the British Library.

For details of other military history titles published by Helion & Company Limited, contact the above address, or visit our website: http://www.helion.co.uk

We always welcome receiving book proposals from prospective authors.

Contents

Glossary iv
Abbreviations used in text v
Introduction vii

1 Motorized Anti-Aircraft Artillery 9
1.1 Self-propelled guns 13
1.2 Motor-towed guns 20
1.3 Tracked self-propelled guns 23
1.4 Searchlight platoons 24
1.5 Motor vehicles versus horses 27

2 Armoured Car Units 31
2.1 Organization and equipment 31
2.2 First blood in the West 35
2.3 The Romanian Front 35
2.4 Lessons learnt 42
2.5 The first expansion 42
2.6 Captured armored cars 48
2.7 The second expansion 52
2.8 Germans drive to the East 56

3 Assault Tank Detachments 68
3.1 Development of armored fighting vehicles 68
3.2 Organization, training and tactical approach 79
3.3 Tanks in action 90

4 Uniforms, Personal Equipment and Weapons 109
Pre-war (parade) uniforms 109
Straps and emblems 109
The *Kraftfahrtruppen* (Motorized Transport Troops) uniform specific elements (1914) 110
Field uniform 110
Headdress 113
Black leather suit 113
Work overalls 113
Armored fighting vehicle crew dress 117
Personal weapons and equipment 117

Afterword 119

Appendices:

I Technical specifications of selected fighting vehicles 123
II Development Timeline of Selected German Motorized Vehicles (1914-1918) 125

Bibliography 126

Glossary

Since the author relied on several German-language sources, it might be prudent to outline the approach to translating and naming German units and vehicle types.

The German formation titles are given their full designation upon the first introduction, with no effort made to produce a German-English hybrid. Thus, for example, the 1st Armoured Motor Machine Gun Platoon is initially rendered as the *Panzer Kraftwagen Maschinengewehr Zug-1 / Pz.Kw.MG.Zug-1* or shortly the 1st Platoon / *Zug 1*.

Ordinal numbers are rendered by using a period in German; thus, the 1st Infantry Division is *1.Infanterie Division* (or, for brevity *1.Inf.Div.*) while the 2nd Tank Assault Detachment is *Sturm Panzer Kraftwagen Abteilung 2,* abbreviated as *Sturm Pz. Abt.* 2 or just *Stuka 2*.

Subordinate units within formations are indicated by Arabic numerals for company-size formations (*1, 2,* etc.) and Roman numerals (e.g. *I, II*) for battalions (*Abteilungen*). The term *Abteilung (Abt.)* is generally translated as 'battalion' when it refers to a combat formation or as 'detachment' when it refers to smaller than battalion units representing a specific branch of arms, e.g. assault tank detachment.

Generally, division and higher commands are indicated by ordinal numbers; regiments, battalions, and separate/independent companies typically have the numerical designator following the unit designator.

When the word 'formation' is used, it refers to a battalion or higher element. The term 'unit' is reserved for company-size elements and smaller. Although the term *Schwadron* is literally translated as 'squadron,' this is actually a troop or company in U.S./U.K. usage.

When the original German terminology is unclear, or a mixture of formations and units is being described, then the term 'elements' is used. The spelling *Truppe* is used for 'troops' in the sense of a whole branch or category, and *Truppen* for a number of individuals.

Throughout this text, italics is used for German terms or names, except Panzer - 'armour', and thus, by extension 'tank' - because of its frequent appearance and familiarity to English-speaking readers.

German vehicle types are consistently presented with their full original designations when first introduced, without any attempt to create a German-English hybrid term. This approach maintains the authenticity and precision of the original terminology, ensuring that readers are acquainted with the exact names used by the German military during the period in question. For instance, the term artillery prime mover is accurately referred to as *Artillerie-Kraftzugmaschine*, while the artillery steam engine tractor is designated as *Dampfzugmaschine*, reflecting the specific terminology.

Given the richness of the text in non-English phrases and technical terms, a special section dedicated to abbreviations has been included at the end of this section.

Photos, images and graphics

This book relies on photographs sourced from a variety of public and private collections, including authors collection of postcards (*postkarten*) and photos (AC), Archiv Axel Oskar Mathieu (AAOM), Bayer Hauptstaatsarchiv (BH), Bundesarchiv Koblenz (BK), Imperial War Museum (IWM), Musée des Deux Guerres Mondiales (BDIC), National Archives and Record Administration (NARA), Patton Museum (PM), RAC Tank Museum (RAC TM), and Stuttgart Hauptstaatsarchiv (SH). All org-charts were drafted by the author.

Geographical names

All geographical names, including names of towns, villages, rivers, mountains and mountain ranges, are given in their original form from 1914-18, but where appropriate, the current geographical names have been placed next to the historical names (e.g. Yuryev/Dorpat, nowadays Tartu).

Linear measurements

Distances and dimensions are given in the metric system of centimetres, meters, and kilometres. Gun calibres below 2cm are specified in millimetres (e.g., 7.92mm), while those above 2cm are listed in centimetres (e.g., 8.0cm).

Abbreviations used in text

Abbr.	*German*	**English**
Abt.	Abteilung	Battalion (Bn.) or Detachment (Det.)
	Armee	Field Army
AK	Armeekorps	Army Corps
AKD	Allgemeines Kriegsdepartement	General War Department
AKK	Armee-Kraftwagen-Kolonne	Army Motor Vehicle (MV) Column
AKP	Armee-Kraftwagen-Park	Field Army MV Park
AKS	Armee-Kraftwagen-Staffeln	Army MV Squadrons
AOK	Armeeoberkommando	Army Command
APK	Artillerie-Prüfungs-Kommission	Artillery Test Commission
Art.	Artillerie	Artillery
Bn.	Bataillon	Battalion
Chefkraft	Chef des Feldkraftfahrwesens	Chief of Field Motor Vehicles
Div.	Division	Division
DKK	Divisions-Kraftwagen-Kolonne	Division MV Column
	Etappen	Field Army Rear Echelon / Sector
	Etappen Inspektion	Rear Echelon Transport Inspections
EKK	Etappen-Kraftwagen-Kolonne	Rear Echelon MV Column
EKP	Etappen-Kraftwagen-Park	Rear Echelon MV Park
ESKA	Etappen-Sanitäts-Kraftfahrzeug-Abteilung	Rear Echelon Mot. Ambulance Det.
	Feldartillerie Regimenter auf Kraftwagen	Field Artillery Regt. (mot.)
FAA	Feld Flieger Abteilung	Field Flier Detachment
	Feldkraftfahrwesen	Mechanical Transport Service
FKK	Feldpost-Kraftwagen-Kolonne	Fieldpost MV Column
FKP	Festungs-Kraftwagen-Park	Fortress MV Park
FKA	Fleisch-Kraftwagen-Kolonne	Fresch Meat (foodstuff) MV Column
Flak	Flugabwehrkanone	Anti-aircraft gun
FKP	Fussartillerie-Kraftzug-Park	Foot (Heavy) Art. MV Park
FMK	Fussartillerie-Munitions-Kolonne	Foot (Heavy) Art. Ammunition Column
G/Gesch.	Geschütz	gun (canon)
	Heeresartillerie Regiment	Independent (reserve) Art. Regt.
Hgr	Heeresgruppe	Army Group
	Heimatheer	Home Army
JKD	Immobiles-Kraftwagen-Depot	Stationary MV Depot
Ikraft	Inspektion des Kraftfahrwesens	Motor Vehicle Inspection
Jasta	Jagdstaffel	Fighter Squadron
	Kommandeur der Kraftfahrtruppen	Field CO of Motorized Troops
	Korps	Corps
KKK	Korps-Kraftwagen-Kolonne	Corps MV Column
	Kraftfahr-Bataillon	MV Transport Battalion
	Kraftfahr-Kolonne	MV Transport Column

Abbr.	***German***	**English**
	Kraftfahrtruppe	Motorized (Transport) Troops
	Kraftwagen-Park	Motor Vehicles Depot
K-flak	Kraftwagenflak	AA motor vehicle
KK	Kraftwagen-Kolonne	motorized column (MC)
KM	Kriegsministerium	Ministry of War
MG	Maschinengewehr	machine gun
MK	Militär Kraftwagen	military motor vehicle
OHL	Oberste Heeresleitung	Army High Command
	Panzerkraftwagen-Maschinengewehr-Abt.	Armoured Motor Machine Gun Det.
	Panzerkraftwagen-Maschinengewehr-Zug	Armoured Motor Machine Gun Platoon
SKA / Sanka	Sanitäts Kraftwagen Abteilung	Medical Motorized Detachment
Sturm Pz. Abt.	Sturm-Panzer-Kraftwagen-Abteilung	Assault Tank Detachment
	Schwere-Kampfwagen-Abteilung	Heavy Assault Tank Detachment
	Staffel	Squadron
	Verkehrstruppen	technical troops
VPK	Verkehrstechnische-Prüfungs-Kommission	Evaluation Commission for Transport Technology
	Zug	Platoon
	Zug	prime mover (vehicle)

Introduction

The story of the Imperial German Motorized Troops examines the evolution of one of the most pivotal yet often overlooked aspects of the German military during the First World War. This book, and its second volume, meticulously covers the organizational development of the motorized troops (Kraftfahrtruppen), tracing their transformation from rudimentary motorized units into more sophisticated and specialized formations by the war's end. The narrative explores the structural changes within these units and also provides a comprehensive examination of the equipment and weaponry that they employed. It provides detailed accounts of the vehicles that were at the forefront of this technological evolution, from the early, experimental vehicles to the few but significant tank designs that emerged from the German war effort. Each chapter highlights how these innovations were born out of necessity and how they were integrated into the broader strategy of the Imperial Army. In addition to the organizational and technical aspects, the book looks at the combat operations of these motorized troops. Through vivid descriptions of key battles and campaigns, readers will gain an understanding of how these units were deployed, the challenges they faced on the battlefield, and their overall impact on the war's outcome. The analysis examines the successes and shortcomings of the German motorized forces, offering insights into why they were ultimately unable to achieve their full potential during the conflict.

What sets this work apart is its rich visual documentation. The book is highly illustrated with many rarely published archive photos, offering a unique visual narrative that complements the text. These images provide an intimate look at the men, machines, and moments that defined the German motorized troops during the Great War. From the dusty roads of the Eastern Front to the muddy trenches of the Western Front, these photographs bring to life the reality of motorized warfare in a way that words alone cannot.

Whether you're a military historian, an enthusiast of early 20th century warfare, or simply curious about the technological and strategic developments of the time, I trust that this book offers a thorough and compelling exploration of a critical, yet underappreciated, chapter in military history.

1
Motorized Anti-Aircraft Artillery

The concept of a truck-mounted self-propelled anti-aircraft (AA) gun had been present as far back as 1906, when the Artillery Proving Commission (*APK*) issued a warning about French advances in balloon technology. In response, the Prussian War Ministry began analyzing measures to counter the potential French threat. Concurrently, the German industry started developing the first models of mobile anti-balloon guns (*Ballonabwehrkanone / BAK*). The first prototype, developed by the German firm Ehrhardt, was presented at the Berlin Auto Exhibition of 1906. This vehicle was equipped with a 5.0cm Rheinmetall L/30 gun (with L/30 referring to the barrel length in calibers of the given gun).

The *Ehrhardt* vehicle was designed to provide high-angle fire against balloons, featuring a gun mounted in a turret with a traverse of 90 degrees on either side of the vehicle's centerline, allowing it to fire at elevations from 0 to 90 degrees. Marketed as a 'panzer automobile for balloon pursuit' (*Panzerautomobil zur Ballonverfolgung*), the vehicle was intended not only for stationary firing at airborne targets but also for chasing them and firing on the move.

The command of the Royal Prussian Army showed interest in this new type of equipment and even conducted field tests. However, these tests revealed numerous flaws in both the gun's design and the self-propelled mount. The most significant criticism was directed at the imperfections in the fuse.

Three years later, during the Frankfurt International Exhibition of 1909, Krupp presented a 7.5cm gun mounted on a motorized vehicle. By January 1910 the Prussian War Ministry had defined the tactical tasks for the use of armored cars and self-propelled anti-aircraft guns within cavalry units, specifically to protect them during offensive operations. This led to calls for new trials, showing interest in more advanced designs. Regarding anti-aircraft guns, the primary requirement from the artillery command was clear—increase their caliber. This decision was made to improve the ballistics and overall effectiveness of the guns.

German industrialists responded swiftly to the Prussian military's call for new artillery guns and vehicles, aligning their developments with the specified requirements and recommendations.

By 1909, Heinrich Ehrhardt had secured a license to produce all-wheel-drive truck chassis with a 70hp, 4-cylinder engine, named *Lafette*, specifically intended for mounting anti-aircraft guns and building armored cars. A new 6.5cm L/35 gun was installed on the vehicle's platform, with ammunition boxes positioned at the rear and behind the driver's seat. The rear box also served as a seat for the crew during transport. To stabilize the gun and maintain horizontal centering during firing, the vehicle was equipped with massive extendable supports. In combat mode, the front and rear seats folded down to provide access to the ammunition. The sides of the vehicle could be lowered to the level of the platform, increasing the usable area of the combat compartment—a design that later became 'classic.'

Simultaneously, Krupp, the largest German military-industrial concern, joined the race to develop anti-aircraft weaponry. Lacking its own automobile production, Friedrich Krupp partnered with the Daimler company, which already had experience in building all-wheel-drive vehicles. In 1908, Daimler introduced the all-wheel-drive Daimler truck (*Daimler Plattformwagen*) with a 52hp, 4-cylinder engine, designed as a weapons carrier. A pedestal-mounted 6.5cm L/35 gun, designed by Krupp, was installed in the middle of the platform behind the driver's cab. While military experts highly praised this gun mount, firing tests yielded unsatisfactory results.

In 1909, Krupp designed and publicly presented a new 7.5cm L/35 motorized gun (with some sources citing L/27, L/28, or L/30). Additionally, in 1908, a new 7.7cm L/27 gun mounted in a rotating turret was introduced, which later became the primary anti-aircraft gun of the German army. The 7.7cm gun, equipped with a semi-automatic breech, was capable of firing up to 20 rounds per minute, though its actual rate of fire in combat conditions was halved—a common issue with almost all anti-aircraft guns of the era.

By 1912, a new semi-armored 70hp Ehrhardt vehicle was built, equipped with a 6.5cm L/35 gun from the 1908 model. Subsequent modifications featured 7.7cm guns of the previously tested L/30 model and the newer L/27 model, all produced by the Rhenish Metal and Engineering Works.

Early self-propelled AA guns

One of the pre-war experimental self-propelled anti-aircraft guns, the *Daimler-Krupp K-Flak Model 1910* (*Krupp* 7.1cm L/30), with its crew taking their assigned positions, ready to repel an air attack. (AC)

A *Rheinmetal* 7.7cm L/27 M.1911 *Ballon-Abwehr-Kanone (BAK)* based on *Lafette* truck chassis, one of the few self-propelled AA guns manufactured before the war's onset, designated to the *VI.Armee* in 1914. (AC)

A makeshift anti-aircraft vehicle (*Presto* based?) from the *I.Armee, Etappen-Kraftwagen-Park* equipped with a captured French *St. Étienne Mle* 1907 machine gun. (AC)

Self-propelled AA guns

Early version of *Kw.14* with a 7.7cm gun (L/27), captured by soldiers of the 3rd Finnish Rifle Regiment on the road to Kopciovo, September 1914, in the Eastern Front. The gun was subsequently repaired at the Putilov Factory in Petrograd, and used by the Russian Army. Note the early production protective shield, and the non-standard, civil registration number. (AC)

An *Ehrhardt Kw.14* is positioned at an airfield in the early days of the war. While the crew prepares to fire, officers are calculating the distance to the plane and the angle at which the gun must be fired. They are using binoculars and a rangefinder (*Entfernungsmesser*) for this purpose. (AC)

An *Ehrhardt Kw.14* photographed in motion during the autumn of 1917. Notable details on the right side include the spare tire and the shell compartment.

In that same year, Section 4 (*Feldartillerie*) of the Artillery Testing Commission (*AKD*) decided to equip the army with self-propelled anti-aircraft guns. New requirements were established for the automotive platforms: they needed to have an all-wheel-drive chassis with wide metal bands on the wheels' rims to improve off-road performance and prevent sinking into soft ground, along with solid rubber tires, a differential lock device, and an engine with at least 70hp. Additionally, the development of specialized vehicles for transporting ammunition was proposed.

The following year, Erhardt and Krupp continued to refine their motorized guns. Engineers at the Erhardt factory improved the 70-horsepower chassis, designing it for dual use as both a platform for an anti-aircraft gun and a base for an armored vehicle. This new model was assigned the factory designation *E-V/4*. Meanwhile, *Daimler* began producing reinforced chassis with a new design featuring a low-mounted frame and a 70-horsepower engine. After building and testing two Krupp-Daimler motorized guns in 1913, it was decided to increase the engine power to 80hp to improve the mobility of the heavy unit, which had a total weight of 7,035 kg. This vehicle was designated as the *K.D.* (*Krupp-Daimler*).

1.1 Self-propelled guns

In 1914, at the request of the Prussian military authorities, Daimler and Erhardt began producing specialized all-wheel-drive automotive chassis to serve as bases for 7.7cm guns from Krupp and Rheinmetall-Erhardt. The initial order called for 80 motorized anti-aircraft guns—40 from each company. This new weapon type was officially designated as *Leichtes Kraftwagengeschütz* M.1914 (*Kw. 14*) and began deployment to the artillery units of the German armies in the summer of 1914.

By the start of the First World War, only six serially produced semi-armored anti-aircraft self-prop guns and 12 horse-drawn 7.7cm AA guns had been delivered to the troops. These widely cited figures likely contributed to the belief that only six mobile guns had been produced by August 1914. However, the actual number was higher, as experimental pre-war vehicles that joined the army were not included in these statistics.

Self-propelled AA guns
An *Ehrhardt Kw.14* from the 29th AA Battery (*K.Flak.29*) based on the tactical markings painted on the bonnet. Note the Imperial eagle emblem on the load box. (AC)

The crew of a *Krupp-Daimler Kw.14* ready to fire the gun. The officer on the right side is using a rangefinder. The vehicle is marked with non-standard version of white Imperial eagle, used by some AA batteries starting from 1917. (AC)

An anti-aircraft artillery detachment from the *VI. Armee* consists of a staff car, a self-propelled anti-aircraft gun (*Krupp-Daimler Kw.14*), and an ammunition lorry. All vehicles are painted *Feldgrau*. (AC)

Self-propelled AA guns
Lorry-mounted AA guns, given sufficient fuel and spare parts, could be quickly repositioned around the front, making them a deadly weapon against both aircraft and tanks, particularly during the Battle of Cambrai.
An *Ehrhardt Kw.14,* viewed from the side, showcases the robust design of this early mobile gun. (AC)

An *Ehrhardt Kw.14* from the *Armee-Abteilung v. Falkenhausen.* Registration number (**F 39**) prepared for action. (AC)

An *Ehrhardt Kw.14* gun registered to *Armee-Abteilung Gaede,* Western Front in 1916, from the 67th AA Battery. (AC)

Of the new six anti-aircraft vehicles, one was distributed to each of the *IV, V, VI,* and *VIII Armee*, with the *VII.Armee* receiving two. While motorized guns accompanied various army corps during the initial German advance, the horse-drawn guns were used to protect key bridges along the Rhine and airship hangars within Germany.

In September 1914 one of the new self-propelled AA guns from the VIII Army was lost, but the remaining guns continued to operate successfully on both the Western and Eastern Fronts, primarily protecting field airfields as part of the field artillery.

By the end of 1914, the number of self-propelled AA guns had increased to 25, with three deployed on the Eastern Front. During this time, the Erhardt company modernized its model by reducing the vehicle's weight: designers removed the gun shield, altered the shape of the armored hood, and replaced the wheels with lighter ones that lacked the metal bands on the rims. Krupp's engineers also modernized and lightened their unit by removing the gun shield. In the fall of 1914, the order for motorized guns was increased to 120 units (Krupp produced 57 serial *Kw.14s* by the end of 1915, although exact figures for Erhardt are not available). Initially, the anti-aircraft vehicles operated in units of one (*K-Flak-Abteilung*), but from 1916, they began to be organized into anti-aircraft batteries (*K-Flak-Batterie*), with two guns per battery.

Beginning in May 1916 the Germans introduced the new abbreviation *K-Flak* or *Kw-Flak* (*Kraftwagengeschütz-Fliegerabwehrkanone*, literally 'vehicle-mounted gun – anti-aircraft cannon'; later *Kraftwagen-Flugabwehrkanone* = 'vehicle – anti-aircraft gun') alongside the old name *BAK*. The official term *Flugabwehrkanone auf Kraftwagen* ('anti-aircraft gun on a vehicle') was also used.

It is important to note that by 8 October 1916 the organizational separation of anti-aircraft artillery from field artillery had been completed. This newly formed branch of service fell under the command of the Air Service (*Fliegertruppen*), which was logical given that anti-aircraft units required distinct firing processes, tactics, and specialized guns and aiming devices compared to field artillery. In the field, anti-aircraft units were placed under the supervision of an officer from the field headquarters (*Armee* or *Korps*). This arrangement extended to anti-aircraft searchlights, which, at the Army Group level, were structured into Anti-Aircraft Groups or *Flakgruppen.*

By early 1917, there were 105 self-propelled guns from Krupp-Daimler and Erhardt, along with one captured Italian vehicle, in service. The primary function of the *Kw. 14* was to provide mobile air defense for strategic targets such as supply depots, command centers, bridges, and key front-line sectors.

In addition to their anti-aircraft role, *Kw.14s* were also employed as anti-tank guns in the war's final year, demonstrating their ability to quickly relocate and counter Allied armored thrusts. Notably, artillery units equipped with *Kw.14s* played a pivotal role in destroying 52 British tanks during the Battle of Cambrai.

By the end of the war, the German armies across all fronts had around 85 automotive anti-aircraft batteries equipped with light guns, a number that was insufficient given the demands of the conflict.

Some sources indicate that at the beginning of 1918, a new self-propelled gun was developed, featuring a 70hp chassis supplied by Erhardt and the 7.62cm *K-Flak* L/31.5 M.1918 gun, manufactured by Henschel & Sohn in Kassel.

Self-propelled AA guns
A *Krupp-Daimler Kw.14* preparing for action. (AC)

A *Kw.14* adorned in a patchwork of yellow clay, brown, green, and field gray camouflage, proudly displays the AA artillery emblem—a winged artillery shell (*Geflugelte Granat*) - on its bonnet. (AC)

The movements of *Kw.14s* between the Western and Eastern Fronts were facilitated by rail transport, which was the quickest and most efficient method for moving heavy military equipment. (AC)

Self-propelled AA guns

Operating open-top *Kw.14s* in winter conditions was extremely challenging due to freezing temperatures and harsh weather. It is worth noting that during the First World War, the Germans did not use winter camouflage (all-white paint) on their military vehicles. (AC)

A commemorative photo of an unidentified anti-aircraft battery, most likely taken in France. (AC)

An anti-aircraft battery of the German corps in Palestine, consisting of two *Krupp-Daimler Kw.14s*, an ammunition truck, and a staff car. Nazareth, April 1918. (AC)

To improve stabilization during firing, German designers once again employed side-support legs to reduce the load on the vehicle's frame.

The gun's design was based on the Russian 7.62cm divisional gun from the Putilov factory, model 1902, which had been adapted for anti-aircraft use. Many of these Russian guns had been captured by the Germans and repurposed, with ammunition production even established in German factories. However, it remains unclear if, or how many of, these machines were deployed by frontline units.

It is certain however that on 19 September 1918 the decision was made to adopt a new 100hp *Krupp-Daimler K.D. I* tractor as a platform for motorized guns. An order was placed for 240 anti-aircraft vehicles, with the first prototype tested in October.

The powerful engine of the *K.D. I* tractor and its massive chassis allowed for a maximum speed of 35km/h and a loaded weight of 11,250 kg. Stabilization on rough terrain was achieved with portable brake blocks, and the vehicle was equipped with a winch and a retractable counterweight at the front. It was not armored.

By the end of the war, the Daimler factory in Stuttgart had built 63 *K.D. I* chassis with 7.7cm Krupp guns. These new anti-aircraft vehicles, including one prototype with a 7.62cm Henschel gun, were tested and received the official army designation *Kw.19*. However, they never reached the front. Most of these vehicles were destroyed in 1920 in accordance with the terms of the Treaty of Versailles, although some were acquired by the Army of the Weimer Republic (*Reichswehr*).

By the war's end, the Germans had 156 self-propelled anti-aircraft guns in service all of types. The total production between 1914 and 1918, including vehicles supplied to German allies, amounted to approximately 200-250 vehicles, of which over 50 were lost in combat.

1.2 Motor-towed guns

By 1916-17, the Entente countries had significantly increased their air operations and began deploying large formations of medium and heavy bombers. The German army urgently needed new, more powerful large-caliber guns. However, the automotive industry did not produce suitable motorized carriages for such guns, necessitating the design of special towed carriages. Mobility for these systems was to be provided by powerful wheeled tractors and artillery haulers.

Between April 1917 and April 1918 the Germans formed 35 batteries armed with 8.0cm L/45 anti-aircraft guns manufactured by Krupp. These guns could engage targets at a horizontal range of 10,100 meters and a vertical range of 6,450 meters, with a firing rate of 10 rounds per minute. The total weight of the installation was 6,800 kg. A total of 74 (or 78) units of these 8.0cm towed guns were produced; however, due to ballistic performance issues, production was halted before the war ended.

In September 1916 *Rheinische Metall- und Maschinenfabrik* delivered the first 8.8cm *K-Zugflak* L/45 M.1916 anti-aircraft gun, mounted on a low-profile heavy trailer. After successful trials, minor modifications were made to the gun, and the second unit was delivered in late November of the same year. These guns were used to form the 101st Motorized Anti-Aircraft Battery. In 1917, four more batteries with M.1916 guns and nine batteries with upgraded M.1917 guns were formed.

Self-Propelled AA Guns
The *Ehrhardt Kw.14*, equipped with a 7.7cm gun, met the mobility requirements even in deep mud due to affixed wheel pads to the circumferences, but struggled to engage high-altitude targets due to its gun's insufficient muzzle velocity, leading to relatively long projectile flight times. (AC)

A *Krupp- Daimler Kw.14,* ready for action, somewhere in France, likely dating to 1916-1917, as indicated by the white Imperial eagle symbol. The registration plate (55K) identifies it as belonging to the 55th AA Battery. (AC)

A *Krupp-Daimler Kw.19,* based on the *K.D.I* tractor chassis, was produced in late 1918. It did not enter service before the Great War ended but was later incorporated into the *Reichswehr* in the early 1920s. (AC)

Heavy AA guns (8.0/8.8. cm)
The combat debut of the *Krupp* 8.0cm *K-Zugflak* L/45 anti-aircraft guns occurred in battles in the Somme area. April 1918. Introduction of heavy AA guns with increased muzzle velocity resulted in a shorter flight time for the shell, which, in turn, allowed for increased rates of fire and a more rapid estimation of necessary firing corrections. The introduction of mechanically timed fuse munitions, shells capable of being set to explode after a given flight time, also enhanced the effectiveness of flak defenses. The marriage of the optical range finder and the mechanical timed fuse allowed gun crews to set the shells to explode at a point in the projectile's flight corresponding to the estimated distance to the target. (AC)

8.8cm anti-aircraft gun on a trailer mount. Western Front, 1917. (AC)

Most, if not all, 8.0/8.8 cm guns were painted with disruptive camouflage, as this requirement was introduced in mid-1918 for all heavy military equipment. (AC)

In April and May 1917 the Artillery Proving Commission (*APK*) approved the first *Krupp* 8.8cm Flak L/45 guns, which were subsequently issued to the 106th Motorized Anti-Aircraft Battery. By the end of the war, 132 of these guns had been delivered to the army, from which the Germans formed 66 batteries. The total weight of the trailer with the gun was 7,300 kg (the *Erhardt* installation was 100 kg lighter).

As already mentioned, due to their considerable weight, these new guns could not be mounted on trucks. Instead, they were affixed to two-axle platform trailers and towed by motorized tractors, which maintained an average speed of about 25km/h on well-maintained roads while pulling the gun trailer.

Initially, the guns were towed by Erhardt trucks, which featured four-wheel drive but lacked off-road capability due to the absence of grippers on the wheels. Four gun crew members could sit on the equipment chest, while three occupied the chest behind the driver's seat. Each of the two ammunition chests could carry 72 shells. All 8.0/8.8cm guns were assigned the 100hp *Krupp-Daimler K.D. I Artilleriezugmaschine* artillery tractor as their towing vehicle. Equipped with a four-speed gearbox, this tractor had superior off-road capabilities. Its large wheels, fitted with shovel-like grippers, allowed it to traverse both smooth and rough terrain. Additionally, a winch on the vehicle's rear facilitated towing the unhooked gun trailer up inclines of up to 45 degrees.

1.3 Tracked self-propelled guns

Notably, German engineers distinguished themselves not only in the development of motorized anti-aircraft artillery but also by creating the world's first tracked self-propelled anti-aircraft vehicles. These were based on the chassis of the *A7V Überlandwagen*, an ammunition carrier that used the suspension system of the *A7V* tank.

At the end of 1917, one of these vehicles was converted into a self-propelled anti-aircraft gun by mounting two *Krupp* 7.7cm Flak L/27 guns on the platform—one at the front and one at the rear. This new vehicle was named the *A7V Flakpanzer*. It was deployed with the 16th Motorized Anti-Aircraft Battery and participated in battles in France early in 1918.

By the end of 1918, two more tracked self-propelled anti-aircraft vehicles were manufactured, forming two additional batteries—the 17th and 18th. These new vehicles were also based on the *A7V Überlandwagen* and were equipped with two captured Russian 76.2cm M.1902/30 guns, adapted for firing at aerial targets, mounted at the front and rear of the platform. Both batteries were sent to the French city of Valenciennes, where the German Army Anti-Aircraft Artillery School was located. This school trained personnel in driving wheeled and tracked vehicles, servicing artillery systems, and conducting anti-aircraft shooting.

1.4 Searchlight platoons

The German army experimented with searchlights as early as 1912, but only by 1914 had independent searchlight platoons (*Scheinwerfer-Züge*) for battlefield illumination been created and subordinated to the Corps of Engineers. Each *Pionier-Bataillon* of an *Armee-Korps* had one searchlight platoon.

In response to the growing number of nighttime aerial raids, the army introduced improved searchlights and sound detectors in 1915. The early searchlights enabled the illumination of attacking aircraft at altitudes of up to 3,000 meters, with later versions extending this range to 6,000 meters.

Heavy AA gun tractors
Initially, 8.0/8.8cm AA guns were towed by *Ehrhardt E-V/4* tractors, which also served as the base for the *Kw.14's*. These vehicles were also used to transport most of the crew and ammunition. (AC)

Since *E-V/4* tractors were produced in limited numbers, some Büssing heavy tractors had to be employed in AA batteries. However, this solution was suboptimal as these vehicles were the only type capable of towing super-heavy siege guns. (AC)

Ultimately, all 8.8cm guns were to be towed by *Krupp-Daimler K.D.I* tractors. A heavy AA battery typically had only two guns, two *KD.I's*, sometimes additional ammunition trucks and required three officers and 50 NCOs and soldiers as personnel. (AC)

Heavy AA gun tractors
All 8.0, 8.8, and 10.5 cm AA guns for medium-altitude targets were mounted on wheeled carriages optimized for weight and size, allowing them to be towed by the *K.D. Is.* (AC)

The heavy AA gun crew was carried in the truck and on the trailer / carriage. Due to a shortage of rubber, both the truck and trailer were fitted with steel-rimmed wheels. The *Daimler Motoren Company* delivered around 274 *K.D. Is* by the end of the war to anti-aircraft batteries. (AC)

A heavy AA detachment from the *VI. Armee* consists of a staff car, 8.8cm AA gun towed by the *K.D. I* tractor, and an ammunition lory. (AC)

The primary advantage of using searchlights was their impact on gun crews' firing methods. By illuminating attacking aircraft, they allowed for a shift from static barrage fire to aimed fire during nighttime attacks, significantly reducing the number of rounds needed to shoot down an aircraft. In 1917, *Scheinwerfer* units were subordinated to air defense, and in February 1918 they were reorganized into independent searchlight batteries, each consisting of four platoons with one searchlight per platoon.

By the end of the war a total of 18 motorized air defense searchlight batteries (*Kraftwagen-Flak-Scheinwerfer-Batterien*) Nos. 451-468 and 87 static air defense searchlight batteries (*Flak-Scheinwerfer-Batterien*) were established. These units served as units safeguarding fortresses and munitions factories. By 1918, there were a total of 718 searchlights, which were horse-drawn, mounted on railroad wagons, static or motorized. A searchlight section typically comprised 2 officers, 38 other ranks, 25 horses, and seven vehicles.

Based on a few surviving photographs, it is evident that many of the searchlight vehicles in Imperial German Army service were captured French trucks, indicating significant limitations in German industry regarding this equipment. Additionally, most of the German-made vehicles were converted from commercial trucks rather than being purposely designed for the anti-aircraft units.

It is worth to mention that heavy trucks (e.g *MAG* type) used in searchlight platoons were also employed in aircraft recovery operations.

1.5 Motor vehicles versus horses

Despite the considerable efforts made during the Great War to modernize and mechanize the German artillery, it largely remained a horse-drawn force.

As the First World War drew to an end, the German artillery possessed around 19,500 field guns and approximately 7,800 heavy guns. By 1918, the personnel count had expanded significantly, with 18,500 officers (up from 1,420 in 1914), 400,000 non-commissioned officers and enlisted personnel (up from 33,250), and 202,500 horses (up from 3,400). In comparison, there were fewer than 20,000 trucks, tractors, and cars in service, at best one-fifth of the equipment available to the Entente forces.

Despite advancements in technology, the field artillery remained reliant on horses. In fact, the number of horses compared to the number of guns in 1918 increased disproportionately compared to 1914. This was primarily due to the escalating need for transportation to accommodate the significantly increased ammunition rates. Additionally, the lower quality of horse fodder meant that the animals could pull less weight, necessitating a higher number of them to carry the same load. Of the 1.27 million horses in the German army during the war, no less than 68 percent were lost.

Static vs. mobile AA guns
Throughout the Great War, mobile (motorized) AA guns remained a minority. The core of the German *Flak* units consisted of field guns, like the 7.7cm *Feldkanone* shown in the photo, adapted to address the urgent need for anti-aircraft defense. The quickest solution was to mount these guns on elevated platforms, known as *Behelfs-Flak* (improvised Flak), to provide the necessary elevation for engaging aircraft. (AC)

While primarily relying on static AA guns, the Germans experimented with various non-standard solutions, including the *A7V Flakpanzer*—the world's first tracked AA vehicle, equipped with two captured Russian 7.62cm M.1902/30 guns. Three such vehicles were produced in 1918. (AC)

Searchlight equipment was critical for both static and mobile AA guns when countering night bombers. While the majority of searchlights were horse-drawn, the German army also possessed a limited number of motorized searchlights, including some captured from the French. (AC)

Horses vs motorized vehicles
Despite the increasing use of motor vehicles, horses remained a crucial part of the war effort, and their contributions were valued by the armies of all the nations involved in the conflict. Motor vehicles were effective on good roads, but on poorer terrain near the front, only horses could get through. The use of horses in the war was a significant logistical challenge, as they required food, water, and care. They were also vulnerable to injury and disease, which further added to the challenges faced by the military.
A heavy field artillery wagon, likely used for carrying munitions, towed by four horses. (AC)

Two-horse light wagons were used to transport supplies. (Photo: Bundesarchive / BB)

Many horse-drawn wagons were of civilian origin, confiscated from local farmers. (AC)

2
Armoured Car Units

2.1 Organization and equipment

Prior to the First World War, the Imperial German Army had shown limited interest in armoured cars, however, early experimentation with such vehicles did take place. The first test occurred in 1906 with an *Austro-Daimler* 45hp model, followed by further trials in 1909 with the *Daimler* 40hp and *Büssing* 32hp during the autumn maneuvers of the 5th Guards Infantry Brigade. These tests demonstrated that while the road-bound vehicles could move quickly, they were severely limited by their inability to traverse rough or cross-country terrain. Consequently, the concept of armored cars was deemed impractical and abandoned. As a result, Germany entered the First World War without any armored cars or developed tactical concepts for their use.

The wartime formation of first German armored car units was largely influenced by the successful and versatile tactics demonstrated by Belgian, British, and Russian armoured cars in the early stages of the war. Particularly noteworthy was their proficiency in swiftly gathering intelligence and providing support to infantry operations. While the Germans did respond to those operations with a few makeshift armored cars, details of these actions are scarce.

The Army High Command (*OHL*) ultimately made a strategic decision to task the domestic industry with the construction of wheel-based armored vehicles. On 27 October 1914 the Prussian War Ministry ordered the *ATK* and *VPK* to devise a comprehensive plan for the development of German-designed armored cars. The War Department (*Allgemeines Kriegsdepartement / AKD*) was also instrumental in shaping this initiative. Given the intention to arm the new vehicles with machine guns, the project fell directly under the supervision of Section A2 (A2 - *Infanterie-Abteilung*) of the *AKD*, which held responsibility for infantry-type armament. The armoured cars were anticipated to participate in reconnaissance and combat engagements with enemy cavalry and infantry lacking artillery support. Their potential use to safeguard the rear during a retreat was also considered.

On 3 November 1914 a collaborative effort yielded a set of 16-point technical requirements, including a 360° rotating turret with a machine gun and an additional rear control post to enable engagement in battle while moving backward. The German decision was to design their vehicles with all-wheel-drive, massive solid rubber tires, three machine guns (with one serving as a reserve), well protected against enemy shells and a radio station onboard. Each vehicle's crew should comprise of ten soldiers: a commander, two drivers, an assistant driver, three machine gunners, and an equal number of assistants.

The military presented designers with seemingly conflicting demands, seeking armoured cars that could achieve high speed and maneuverability while ensuring reliable crew protection and substantial armament. Striking a compromise between these conflicting requirements proved challenging. Consequently, the German vehicles proved more powerful than their British or Russian counterparts but were also more complex, heavy, and expensive.

After receiving approval from the War Ministry, the Daimler, Ehrhardt, and Büssing companies secured a production order for just three armored vehicles, each company one. Daimler and Ehrhardt were chosen due to their extensive experience developing all-wheel-drive self-propelled AA guns and heavy military trucks, whose chassis could serve as a base for armored cars. Two models, the *Krupp-Daimler Plattformwagen* and *Ehrhardt Plattformwagen E-V/4*, were selected, both equipped with additional stern controls to minimize design and development time. Büssing was chosen based on its experimental heavy all-wheel-drive chassis developed before the war, which had not yet entered serial production.

On 28 October 1915 Daimler completed the construction of the first armored car, the *Panzerwagen Daimler* M.1915. Trials of the vehicle commenced immediately, and by 10 December the Transport and Weapons Testing Commissions reported its acceptance for combat duties.

The *Ehrhardt* company finalized the construction of the *Ehrhardt Plattformwagen E-V/4* M.1915 in mid-October 1915. Trials for the vehicle were conducted concurrently with the Daimler armored car, but Ehrhardt was officially delivered to the army only on 21 March 1916.

Meanwhile, on 2 February 1916, the General Command of the Guard Corps (*Generalkommando der Gardekorps*) initiated the establishment of the 1st Armored Motor Machine Gun Platoon (*Panzer-Kraftwagen-Maschinengewehr-Zug 1 / Pz.Kw.MG.Zug-1* or shortly the 1st Platoon / *Zug 1*), which was operational on 21 February. Initially, the *Zug-1* was reinforced with a light Belgian

German makeshift fighting vehicles
A 1.5-ton truck, likely a *Benz BL.10* model, has been outfitted with two captured Maxim machine guns, indicating a makeshift yet effective adaptation for mobile firepower. The scene includes gunners stationed around the vehicle and a motorcyclist nearby. Eastern Prussia, 1914. (AC)

A staff car from *Etappen-Kraftwagen-Park 2,* armed with an *MG 08*, photographed in Belgium or France in 1915. This adaptation suggests the increasing need for protection and readiness even within support units, as the war's front lines were often fluid and unpredictable. (AC)

A makshift fighting vehicle equipped with a captured French *St. Étienne Mle* 1907 machine gun. (AC)

The unarmored fighting vehicle (*MG Wagen* M.1914) was based on a *Daimler* car and equipped with MG 08 machine guns, along with a substantial ammunition supply. (AC)

armored car, *Minerva* (*Radpanzer Minerva* M.1914), captured in the battles of 1914 in Flanders. Another similar *Minerva* arrived in the unit from the 5th Reserve Motor Vehicle Park (*Ersatz-Kraftwagen-Park 5*) on 8 May 1916.

The *Büssing A5P* M.1915 became the largest and heaviest combat vehicle of the 1st Platoon, featuring an extravagant appearance with almost identical front and rear parts of the armored vehicle. Due to prolonged construction, refinement, and trials, it was officially accepted into service on 22 May 1916. The vehicle reached the 1st Platoon's location on 19 June 1916, completing the unit's armored car fleet, supplemented by several trucks and staff cars. The combat-ready 1st Platoon was assigned the 7th Reserve Corps (*VII. Reserve Korps*) operating on the Western Front.

Armored car units / Western Front 1916
An unarmed ex-Belgian *Minerva* armored car in German hands. The photo was probably taken in early 1916, as the presence of snow suggests, and the landscape and building in the background suggest that it may have been taken in the Ardennes region rather than in Belgium's lowlands. The armored car appears to be part of *Pz.Kw.MG.Zg.1.* (AC)

An *Ehrhardt* M.1915 and *Daimler* M.1915, in the background, of the German 1st Platoon (*Pz.Kw.MG.Zg-1*). The second vehicle was based on the chassis of a *Kw.14.* The photo was taken in May 1916 at Sivry-sur-Meuse while the platoon operated on the Western Front. At this stage of war, vehicles were marked only with registration numbers B-1593 - *Ehrhardt*, B-1594 - *Daimler* and B-1595 - *Büssing*. (AC)

The sheer size of the German armored cars of the 1st Platoon is evident in this view of three vehicles (from left to right: *Daimler* M.1915, *Ehrhardt* M.1915, and *Büssing A5P* M.1915) and their 29 crewmen. Photo taken in May 1916 at Buchsweiler (Bouxwiller). (AC)

2.2 First blood in the West

The 1st Platoon faced its first combat mission during the Battle of Verdun on 6 March 1916, on the Brabant-Samogneux road. On that day, the German attack on the west bank of the Meuse made slow but steady progress, capturing Forges, Regnéville, and the Bois des Courbeaux. During this operation, *Daimler* and *Minerva* were assigned to cover the flank as the *37th Inf. Regt.* Just before the attack, both German vehicles moved towards Samogneux and initiated fire on French positions in the town of Regnéville. During the battle, the *Daimler* sustained several hits from French small arms, but the bullets failed to penetrate the armor. The heavy *Daimler* reversed first, followed by the light *Minerva*. The German armored cars fired 4,100 rounds from machine guns at the enemy.

In the subsequent weeks, the 1st Platoon faced downtime due to several breakdowns. The *Daimler* experienced a carburetor failure, necessitating a seven-day wait for a replacement. The *Minerva* required repairs to the rear axle and clutch. During this waiting period, additional repairs and upgrades were performed on the armored vehicles.

On 19 June the 1st Platoon received orders to move to Upper Alsace under the command of Army Division B (*Armee Abteilung Gaede*). Initially, the Platoon was transported by rail to the city of Müllheim in Baden, falling under the command of the 8th Reserve Division (*8. Ersatz-Division*), and only on 28 June was it relocated to the town of Buxweiler (Buchsweiler), behind the frontline.

On 15, 18 and 19 July 1916, during a reconnaissance near Hirtzbach, the German cars fired upon enemy positions. On 17 August they came under fire at Pfetterhausen.

By the end of September the Platoon had engaged in several reconnaissance operations, primarily of a training nature rather than intense combat. On 18 September the German vehicles once again fired on French positions, and on 28 September they advanced toward the village of Largitzen.

Technical issues with the machines persisted, and the enemy appeared not significantly affected by skirmishes, given the distance of machine gun fire from 1,500-2,000 meters.

2.3 The Romanian Front

On the night of 27 August 1916 Romania, previously neutral, declared war on Austria-Hungary. Subsequently, its army initiated an offensive in Transylvania, advancing through the Carpathian Mountains. In a brief span, they seized control of Brașov, Făgăraș, and Miercurea Ciuc and approached the outskirts of Hermannstadt (nowadays Sibiu). The swift Romanian progress raised concerns among the Central Powers, prompting substantial reinforcements to the region.

Field Marshal August von Mackensen led the first counterattack with a multinational force comprising Germans, Bulgarians, and Ottomans. Finally, the overall command was shifted to Erich von Falkenhayn, who initiated a massive counterattack on 18 September.

One month later, the decision was made to strengthen the advancing German forces with the reinforced 1st Armored Motor Machine Gun Platoon (*Pz.Kw.MG.Zug-1*), comprised three German heavy armored cars (*Daimler, Ehrhardt,* and *Büssing*), two former Belgian light cars (*Minervas*), three trucks (*Daimler, NAG, and Horch*), an auto workshop mounted on a *NAG* truck chassis with a trailer, and a staff car (*Wanderer*).

Armored car units / Western Front 1916
While early armored cars were relatively primitive, slow and heavy compared to later designs, they represented an important step in the evolution of armored warfare tactics. (AC)

During the spring of 1916, the 1st Platoon was photographed on the Western Front, at Sivry-sur-Meuse, outfitted with four armored cars, each of a distinct type. The upper photo depicts the construction disparities among the *Daimler, Ehrhardt,* and *Büssing* models. (AC)

An ex-Belgian *Minerva*, now equipped with an MG 08 and assigned to the 1st Platoon, is identifiable by its bonnet tactical markings (*P.M.G.Z.1*) and the Iron Cross symbol painted on the rear of the armored body. The photo was taken in mid-1916. (AC)

Armored car units / Western Front 1916

The 1st Platoon trio: the first is *Büssing A5P* M.1915 - the heaviest and largest German armored car, and alongside is the prototype *Ehrhardt*. The furthest vehicle is a *Daimler* with a cylindrical turret instead of the built-up superstructure of the original. It was one of three *Daimler* prototypes that did not reach production. Photo taken in Buchsweiler (Bouxwiller). (AC)

A *Büssing A5P* M.1915. A staged photo, taken during the summer of 1916 in the surroundings of the city of Bouxwiller, Alsace, France. (AC)

A modified version of the ex-Belgian *Minerva,* boasting increased height, features a noticeable addition: a small ladder to facilitate easier crew boarding. Behind the captured car, a heavy *Büssing* is visible. This photo was likely captured at Buchsweiler (Bouxwiller) in 1916. (AC)

On 18 October 1916 the 1st Detachment was redeployed to Transylvania and disembarked in Hermannstadt, falling under the command of the *IX. Armee*. After covering a 120 kilometer march, the detachment established its presence in Brașov (Kronstadt). Until 26 October the 1st Platoon remained under the command of the *IX. Armee*, after which it underwent a division into three groups, each assigned to a different corps. Between 19 and 25 October the *Daimler* and *Minerva* operated under the Alpine Corps (*Alpenkorps*), tasked with supporting pioneers in clearing blockades on the mountain road and patrolling a six-kilometer stretch.

On 21 October, as the *Daimler* and *Minerva* vehicles exited a tunnel near the village of Riu Vadului, both cars faced a barricade and came under fire from Romanian infantry. The Germans retaliated and pulled back. Overnight, soldiers of the 2nd Light Infantry Regiment cleared the road, and the following evening, the *Minerva* advanced to a destroyed bridge, followed by the *Daimler*. Until 25 October both armored vehicles engaged in firefights with the Romanians and, subsequently, returned to Hermannstadt.

On 23 October the *Ehrhardt* joined the cavalry corps of General Eberhard von Schmettow (*Kavalleriekorps Eberhard von Schmettow*), while the *Büssing* was assigned to the 1st Reserve Corps (*1. Reserve Korps*). Both car sub-units carried out reconnaissance missions but, due to inadequate terrain conditions, were finally recalled to Kronnstadt.

On 26 October the entire 1st Platoon shifted under the command of Schmettow's corps, embarking on a march to the distant Hatzeg, covering a distance of 124km. Along the way, the rear axle of the *Büssing* malfunctioned, sending the vehicle for repairs to the factory in Brunswick, Germany. By 9 November the remaining elements of the 1st Platoon were transferred to Petrosani, but technical issues emerged during the journey, rendering the *Daimler* inoperable. Two days later, the sole combat-ready *Ehrhardt* initiated reconnaissance operations as a component of the 4th Cuirassier Regiment (*Kürassier Regt. 4*) within the 7th Cavalry Division (*7.Kavallerie Div.*). On 14 November the *Ehrhardt* became involved in a skirmish with a Romanian cavalry patrol, supported by two infantry companies, during a reconnaissance mission.

The 1st Platoon proceeded to Bumbeşti-Jiu, where the malfunctioning *Daimler* underwent repairs. The 1st Platoon was subsequently assigned to the 2nd Cuirassier Regiment (*Kürassier Regt. 2*) of the 6th Cavalry Division (*6.Kavallerie Div.*), and actively participated in successful reconnaissance missions and minor skirmishes.

On 16 November the 1st Platoon had been elevated to a detachment and renamed to the 1st Armored Motor Machine Gun Detachment (*Panzer Kraftwagen Maschinengewehr Abteilung 1*). Two days later, it set course for Craiova, with only the *Daimler* engaging in combat operations, as other vehicles encountered successive severe breakdowns.

On 20 November the *Ehrhardt* experienced transmission failure and was transported to Germany. On 1 December the *Daimler*'s engine malfunctioned, and a week later, it was also sent back to its homeland. Both *Minerva* armored cars also required repairs, rendering all combat vehicles non-operational.

Despite numerous successes, it is accurate to note that the German armored car crews in Romania faced more challenges with technical issues than with the enemy.

Armored car units / Western Front 1916
Based on the chassis of the *Kw.14*, the Daimler company built the M.1915 armored car. The armor comprised chrome-nickel stainless steel plates securely fastened to the frame, offering limited defense against small arms fire and artillery shrapnel. The engine, housed in the front compartment, was a 4-cylinder gasoline unit producing 80hp. The vehicle featured a 4x2 wheel arrangement across two axles, with the rear axle sporting four tires to accommodate the additional weight of the rear armor, weaponry, ammunition, and crew.

A *Daimler* M.1915 in the rear, preparing for a combat mission. A turret was installed on the roof, giving the gunner an optimal firing angle above the vehicle. Armament consisted of three 7.92mm MG-08 water-cooled machine guns. Later, it was converted into an armored radio vehicle. (AC)

The *Ehrhardt* and *Daimler* (in the background) during a break near the Meuse Valley in April 1916. (AC)

Armored car units / Western Front 1916
In the second half of 1916, the 1st Platoon, equipped with its four cars, was moved to Alsace under the command of Army Division B (*Armee Abteilung B*), where it had engaged in several reconnaissance operations, primarily of a training nature rather than intense combat. Technical issues with the machines persisted, and the enemy appeared unaffected by the armored car operations.
The *Daimler* M.1915 and *Ehrhardt* M.1915 on the Western Front in the summer of 1916. (AC)

The *Büssing A5P* M.1915 in Alsace, close to the Swiss border in September 1916. (AC)

The *Ehrhardt* M.1915. This photo was taken at Buchsweiler (Bouxwiller) in 1916. (AC)

The personnel of the 1st Detachment departed Romania on 2 December 1916, reaching Berlin a week later, where they joined the 5th Reserve Machine Gun Company of the Guards Corps (*5. Ersatz-Maschinengewehr-Kompanie des Garde-Korps*).

2.4 Lessons learnt

After safely wintering and undergoing technical repairs in the rear, on 18 March 1917 the 1st Detachment came under the command of the Supreme General-Governor of Antwerp. During their stay in Belgium, the armored cars were relatively inactive, abstaining even from rear-area patrols and instead focusing on marksmanship training, driving, and mastering radio communication. The unit's personnel expanded to 72 soldiers, comprising five officers and 67 enlisted ranks.

In April one *Minerva* was decommissioned and replaced by a French armored car *Peugeot (Société Anonyme des Automobiles et Cycles Peugeot)*. It was captured from Belgian volunteers in Russia near the village of Svystelnyky in Galicia.

In July the 1st Detachment returned to Berlin. The intensive training in Belgium proved valuable, as the personnel of the only German armored car unit became the foundation for the intended expansion of the armored mobile force.

In the Spring of 1917 the decision was made to establish new armored car units, intending to equip them with new German and, if necessary, captured vehicles. Given the relatively higher reliability of the *Ehrhardt* model, an order for 12 new such vehicles was placed. The primary technical requirements remained consistent with the M.1915 model, with a recommendation to reduce weight and dimensions based on lessons from the Romanian campaign, where excessive weight hindered mobility and maneuverability.

The first two new *Ehrhardt* armored cars, model *E-V/4* M.1917, were delivered out of the factory on 17 July 1917.

2.5 The first expansion

On 9 June 1917 Section A2 of the *Kriegsministerium* announced the establishment of five new armored car machine gun platoons (*Panzerkraftwagen-Maschinengewehr-Zug / Pz.Kw.M.G.Zug. / P.K.M.G.Z.*) numbered from 2 to 6.

The organizational structure of these independent platoons closely resembled that of similar units in the Russian or British armies. The formation of battalions and divisions was never viable due to the limited number of armored vehicles throughout the war,

Each platoon comprised two officers and 37 enlisted men, including four machine gunners, two radio operators, and one driver. Their equipment included two *Erhardt* M.1917 armored cars, two trucks, one car repair shop, and one staff car. The two additional *Erhardts* (Nos. 11 and 12), initially intended as reserve, eventually joined the 1st Detachment.

The formation of the 2nd Platoon (*Pz.Kw.M.G.Zug. 2/P.K.M.G.Z.2*) commenced on 15 June, even before the first new *Erhardts* were shipped from the factory. The training lasted until 14 September 1917. From 20 February to September 1918 the *2.Zug* was based on the Eastern Front, and subsequently, until 2 November, on the Western Front.

Armoured car units / Romanian Front 1916
An *Ehrhardt* M.1915 of the 1st Platoon. The photo was taken in the autumn of 1916, close to Lainici Monastery, while the platoon was destined for the Romanian Front. Note early markings composed of black Iron Crosses painted on white rectangle. (AC)

In October 1916 the *Daimler* M.1915 became part of General von Schmettow's cavalry corps deployed in East Wallachia on the Romanian Front. Note the unit markings (*P.Kr.M.G.Z.1*) indicating the 1st Platoon, as well as the registration number (B-1594), which was inherited from the *Armee Abteilung B* of the Western Front. This number was retained throughout the entire Romanian campaign. (AC)

A *Daimler* M.1915 (B-1594) of the 1st Platoon (*P.K.M.G.A. 1*). Photo taken in November 1916, in Transylvania. On the front plate, the Iron Cross emblem is clearly visible. (AC)

Interestingly, on 19 July the German Army High Command (*OHL*) requested the transfer of the 1st Detachment and the 2nd Platoon to the Middle East for participation in the Yildirim Operation. Soldiers were already provided with uniforms and cork helmets suitable for the climatic conditions, but the expedition plans were soon abandoned, as the roads in Syria were too bad for armored cars.

The 3rd Platoon (*Panzerkraftwagen-Maschinengewehr-Zug 3*) completed its formation on 25 October 1917, near Berlin in Wünsdorf. It was assigned to the *XIV. Armee* in Italy from 14 November 1917 to 24 February 24 1918. During the initial march of the *Zug 3* to Udine, from 14 to 20 November 1917, the unit experienced the customary breakdowns of its vehicles. Following repairs, on 26 November, the *3. Zug* moved to the distant Vittorio Veneto, 80 kilometers away. It arrived after the front line stabilized, which significantly limited its combat potential. A period of several months with low activity was utilized for training personnel who took control of four new *Lancia-Ansaldo 1Z* armored cars captured from the Italians during the recent Battle of Caporetto, also known as the Twelfth Battle of the Isonzo, which occurred between 24 October and 10 November 1917.

On 25 December 1917 an order from the Army High Command (*OHL*) stated that the prevailing circumstances on the (static) front did not allow for the use of armoured cars, and the armoured cars should remain at the disposal of the *OHL*.

In late February 1918 the 3rd Platoon was eventually deployed to the Western Front, arriving on 4 March. Initially engaged in anti-aircraft defense near the town of Sen-Aman, it later took on the responsibility of guarding the frontline road. On 21 March the platoon moved to Masni, then to Estrée, Artois, Somme, Armentières, and Château du Bois.

Its first battle occurred on 13 April on the road near the town of Merville. The platoon cooperated with the 3rd Bavarian Bicycle Battalion (*Königlich-Bayerisches-Radfahrer-Bataillon 3*). Two *Erhardts* dispersed French infantry, but one vehicle sustained damage from enemy artillery fire. While evacuating, the transmission failed on another car, which acted as a tow truck. Consequently, the platoon focused solely on anti-aircraft defense in the towns of Ruch, Grua, Laventie, and Lille. On 21 April the unit was sent from Lille to the Eastern Front (for more detail see section below).

The formation of the 4th Platoon (*Panzerkraftwagen-Maschinengewehr-Zug 4*) was finalized on 10 November 1917, while the 5th and 6th Platoons were completed in late January 1918. All of them were initially based in Wünsdorf.

On 20 February the personnel and equipment of these three armoured units were transported by rail to the Russian front, arriving in German-occupied Livonia near Riga on 24-25 February. All of them were assigned to the 1st Cavalry Division (*1. Kavallerie Div.)* within the *VIII.Armee* and tasked with the mission to capture a railway section and cut off train traffic between Revel and Petrograd. Unfortunately, this task was not accomplished, with German historians attributing the lack of success to unfavorable weather conditions, including heavy snow and frost. The platoons' activities were confined to patrols on rear roads and the ice of Lake Peipus, along with daily radio communication sessions with the command. The winter patrols resulted in many challenges, such as getting stuck in deep snow, falling into pits on roads, and sustaining damage to springs and transmission elements in snowdrifts. By the end of March 1918 nearly all vehicles were undergoing repairs in Yuryev/Dorpat (nowadays Tartu), remaining inactive until the autumn. Only in late September were the 4th and 5th Platoons transferred to Little Russia (Malorossiya).

Armored car units
A *Büssing* photographed in the spring of 1917 upon its return from the Romanian campaign. The Transylvanian campaign proved that the *A5P* M.1915 was too massive and unwieldy to be the future main armored fighting vehicle of the combat motorized formations. (AC)

The first expansion (above and top next page)
As the *Erhardt* M.1915 demonstrated somewhat greater reliability than *Daimler* and *Büssing*, an order was placed for 12 new *Erhardt* vehicles. The new model (M.1917) largely echoed the design principles of its M.1915 predecessor; however, modifications were made to the front and rear sections of the hull, resulting in slight material savings and a modest reduction in vehicle weight. (AC)
Six brand-new *Ehrhards* M.1917 parked in the yard of Wünsdorf Barracks during the summer of 1917. The two unmarked vehicles on the left have not yet been allocated, while the two in the middle (in the larger photo) belong to the 3rd Platoon. The two on the right are designated for the 2nd Platoon. (AC)

Armoured car units. Italian Front 1917 (above and next page)
An *Erhardt* M.1917 of the 3rd Platoon in Italy, Vittorio Vento, 27 November 1917 in attendance for the *Chefkraft's* arrival and subsequent inspection. All vehicles of 3rd Platoon were painted in field gray. Contrary to the staff car, no armored vehicles are marked with the Imperial eagle emblem. Instead, fighting vehicles have tactical markings identifying the *P.Kr.MG.Zug 3* (*Panzerkraftwagen Maschinengewehr Zug 3*) and registration numbers starting from K (K 2486) which was used by the Western Front *Küstenverteidigung* (Coastal Defense). (AC)

The strategic situation on the Eastern Front in February 1918 underwent a fundamental change. Although the Bolsheviks had not yet signed a peace treaty with their adversaries, the old Imperial Russian Army practically ceased to exist. After the breakdown of the Soviet-German peace negotiations in Brest-Litovsk on 18 February, the German offensive, codenamed *Faustschlag* (Hammer Blow), began. It officially concluded on 3 March with the signing of a peace treaty in Brest-Litovsk between representatives of Soviet Russia and the Central Powers. By 2 April 1918 the Germans had captured over 82,000 soldiers and officers of the Russian army, seizing a significant amount of weaponry, including around 800,000 rifles, about 10,000 machine guns, 4,381 guns, 1,203 mortars, 152 aircraft, 1,278 cars, 100 million cartridges, and about 3 million shells. Although armored cars were not included in these statistics, the Russians lost several dozen of them. Most were abandoned in positions and on the roadsides, with many taken to German automotive workshops. In Dvinsk alone, in February 1918, the Germans captured at least five freshly repaired armored vehicles, including two gun cars manufactured at the *Izhorsky* plant.

2.6 Captured armored cars

The intense combat in the West and East, coupled with the German automotive industry's inability to manufacture another batch of armored cars, compelled the Imperial army to formulate a new plan focused on expanding armored car units. The new strategy centered on the widespread incorporation of captured fighting vehicles.

While the first 'war booty' vehicles were captured in the West, the onset of trench warfare in 1915 limited such opportunities. Conversely, as the war in the East maintained a maneuverable character, it also offered numerous opportunities to capture the enemy's armored cars.

From 1914 to 1917, the Russian War Department procured approximately 500 armored cars from England and France. In addition, over 200 vehicles of foreign and domestic origin were armored within Russia itself. The Russians also received support from small British and Belgian expeditionary armored detachments, initially shipped to Archangelsk, from which they were moved to the frontline. Such a significant influx of armored cars into the East had to result in many vehicles being lost in action and recovered by the Germans.

The first two Russian-built armored cars of the *Izhorsky-Hotchkiss* type fell into the hands of the Germans during the battles near Vilnius in August 1915. They came under the control of the 1st Auxiliary Workshop (*Hilfswerkstatt 1*) of the 10th Rear-Sector Motor Park (*Kraftwagen-Motor-Park*). Due to heavy damage, neither of these machines participated in combat operations on the German side.

In May 1916 the Russian army initiated a large-scale operation known as the Brusilov Offensive. A noteworthy aspect of the Russian army's tactics during the offensive was the widespread use of armored car units.

In September 1916, as the Brusilov operation neared its conclusion, the Germans succeeded in capturing a Belgian *Peugeot Type 153* M.1914 near the village of Svistelnyky. It was retrieved from the battlefield under machine gun fire and, after refurbishing, integrated into the 1st Detachment. In 1918, the *Peugeot* was transferred to the newly formed 8th Platoon (*Zug 8*).

During the unsuccessful summer offensive led by Kerensky in 1917, the Germans managed to disable or capture dozens of armored vehicles. Many of these vehicles were in working condition, often abandoned only due to minor malfunctions or a lack of gasoline.

Interestingly, in July 1917, what was likely the first armored car duel in history occurred. According to just one British publication a British Royal Naval Air Service (RNAS) armored car unit supported Russian attacks in the Brzezany sector. They conducted raids down the main road to enfilade enemy trenches and encountered the *Büssing* armored car of the 1st Detachment at a distance of 550 meters. Both sides opened fire, causing no damage, but the German vehicle eventually reversed into its own lines.

On the Northern Front, Russian losses occurred among the armored units defending the naval fortress of Emperor Peter the Great in Revel. Several *Garford*-type armored gun vehicles were knocked out and captured during battles near Riga in the summer of 1917. Moreover, in the Moonsund archipelago islands, two gun-armored vehicles of the *Pierce-Arrow* type ended up in German hands.

Captured armored cars / Italian Front 1917
Ex-Italian *Lancias 1Z* of the 3rd Platoon built on the chassis of the 25/35-hp light truck, which featured pneumatic tires with dual tires at the rear. Ansaldo, an engineering firm based in Turin, undertook the construction of these armored cars. Hence, they were sometimes referred to as *Ansaldos* or Ansaldo Armored Cars. The design layout was relatively conventional. The most notable feature was the small turret mounted atop the larger turret, which was equipped with a machine gun. A crew of six men manned the vehicle. Note the hull markings G1/G3, which stood for for *Gefangenwagen 3* ('Captured vehicle 3'). (AC)

A transport truck from the 3rd Platoon photographed in Italy in 1917. Take note of the registration number (K 2088), with the K prefix assigned to *Küstenverteidigung* (Coastal Defense). This formation was initially allocated for homeland coastal defense, but by 1914, most of its units had been transferred to the Western Front. (AC)

Armored car units. Captured vehicles (above and top next page)
A *Lancia 1Z* from the 3rd Platoon. It's worth noting that besides the tactical markings (*P.K.M.G.Z.3.*) painted on the bonnet, both vehicles also bear Iron Cross symbols on their sides. Such placement of the Prussian national markings was distinct among all captured armored cars. Interestingly, the second vehicle also features a scarcely visible G2 markings. The car is probably in the process of being prepared for service with the 10th Platoon. (AC)

A Russian armored car, an *Austin III,* being repaired in the autumn of 1918 at unknown stationary workshop. During the renovation, the vehicle was repainted gray-green with clearly visible Imperial Army markings. (NARA)

2.7 The second expansion

According to various estimates, during the First World War, the Central Powers managed to capture between 100 and 150 enemy armored cars on various fronts. Most of these captured vehicles were sent to Germany, specifically to the Immobile Automobile Depot 8 (*JKD 8*) in Berlin-Schöneberg, which was responsible for handling captured technology. Only a few armored vehicles were retained on the front to reinforce armored car platoons in the field.

Among the captured vehicles that ended up in German hands were armored cars of British origin (*Austin / Armstrong-Whitworth / Lanchester / Rolls-Royce*), Belgian, French (*Peugeot*), Italian (*FIAT / Lancia*), Russian (*Izhorsky / Putilov*), and even American (*Ford*). These vehicles were equipped with various types of engines, armed with calibers unusual for Germans, and characterized by highly individualized driving parameters. Although they could have been used to form German motorized units, their operational effectiveness would have been significantly limited due to the lack of standardization.

However, confronted with the incapacity to manufacture home-made armored cars, the

German military authorities took action on 24 February 1918, by initiating the establishment of five new armoured car platoons to be outfitted with captured vehicles. On 25 March the Prussian Ministry of War endorsed this initiative and issued the corresponding order for formation to commence on 5 April.

On 20 June 1918 the establishment of the 7th and 8th Platoons (*Panzerkraftwagen-Maschinengewehr-Zug 7 & 8*) commenced. The *Zug 7*, comprising two officers and 25 enlisted personnel, was equipped with two ex-Belgian armored *Minervas* M.1916. Unlike their previous role primarily for reconnaissance, this time the *Minervas* were the sole armored vehicles in the *Zug 7*, tasked with a variety of duties. However, due to their limited firepower and lack of radio equipment, their effectiveness in combat was limited. In July 1918 *Zug 7* was deployed to the Eastern Front, where fighting had ceased following Russia's exit from the war. Despite this, German forces remained to protect their interests against Bolshevik forces and ensure the delivery of promised food supplies from Ukraine to Germany.

It was not until 12 September 1918 that most German armored platoons were redeployed to the Western Front. *Zug 7* was directed to Upper Alsace. Initially slated to support the Prince Rupprecht Army Group against British forces, this plan was later canceled. Instead, like other platoons, *Zug 7* was primarily used for rear patrols and as mobile anti-aircraft defense. Furthermore, lacking radio equipment, *Zug 7's* utility was further limited as the sole German armored car platoon.

The 8th Platoon (two officers, 28 enlisted personnel) was equipped with ex-French *Peugeot*, transferred from the 1st Detachment, and an *Armstrong-Whitworth-FIAT*. In addition to fighting vehicles, both units had two trucks and one staff car each.

On 12 September both platoons (*7* & *8*) were deployed to the Ukrainian front, but there is no information about their combat operations in the East.

In late Autumn 1918, *Zug 8* was transferred to the Western Front. However, due to a railway accident near Trier, both its armored cars became inoperable. The 8th Platoon returned to Wünsdorf and was re-equipped with an *Armstrong-Whitworth-FIAT* only in November 1918, which coincided with the war's end.

The 9th Platoon (*Panzerkraftwagen-Maschinengewehr-Zug 9*) was formed towards the very end of the war, on 10 November 1918. It consisted of two officers and 45 enlisted personnel, along with two heavy *Garford* armored cars manufactured at the *Putilov Plant*, two trucks, one auto workshop, and a staff car. *The Garfords* were armed with Russian 7.62cm cannons, for which the Germans lacked ammunition; thus, they were re-armed into German-calibre 7.92mm machine guns. *Zug 9* was not used in combat operations during the war.

The 10th and 11th Platoons (*Panzerkraftwagen-Maschinengewehr-Zug 10 & 11*) were established on 21 August 1918, and from 30 August until the end of the war they were based on the Western Front. Each platoon had two officers and 37 enlisted personnel, along with two ex-Italian *Lancias 1Z* and the standard set of motor vehicles, including trucks and a staff car.

Additionally, at the end of the war, a reserve training company (*Reserve-Übungskompanie*) was formed in Wünsdorf. It included three officers and 17 enlisted personnel, with 65 soldiers undergoing training in the rotating staff. Three captured armored vehicles (*Austins?*) and, a truck and a staff car were used as training vehicles.

The formal announcement to halt the further formation of armored units using captured vehicles was made by Section A2 of the *Kriegsministerium* only on 27 October 1918.

Armored car units / Eastern Front 1918
The vast, open terrain of Eastern Europe, where paved roads were available, was well-suited for the use of armored cars. These vehicles could quickly move across the battlefield to support infantry operations by exploiting breakthroughs, harassing retreating forces, and securing key locations.
A photograph of an *Ehrhardt* M.1917 from the 6th Platoon, distinguished by the tactical markings of the *P.Kr.M.G. Zug 6* on its engine bonnet, as it travelled along the road towards Dorpat in Russian (present-day Estonia) in March 1918. Note the radio mast in use. (NARA)

Two *Ehrhardt* M.1917 vehicles from the 4th Platoon photographed likely on the Eastern Front during the summer of 1918. Note that while the drivers wear all-leather apparel and a soft headdress, most of the crew is dressed in standard *feldgrau* field uniforms and steel helmets. (AC)

Armored car units / Eastern Front 1918

A *Ehrhardt* M.1917 of the 2nd Platoon, belonging to the German forces in Russia, known as the *Deutsches Besatzungsheer* (1917-1918). The photo was likely taken in Kyiv during the summer of 1917. (AC)

An *Ehrhardt* M.1917, belonging to the 1st Armoured Car Detachment on the Eastern Front, bears the number 1 on its bonnet along with a registration number (DB-), signifying its affiliation with the German occupying army in Russia. (AC)

An *Ehrhardt* M.1917, still bearing the registration GG-0794 (General Government of Belgium), seen in action on the Russian / Ukrainian Front during the spring of 1918. (AC)

2.8 Germans drive to the East

Following the German-Soviet peace treaty signing in Brest-Litovsk on 3 March 1918 combat activities on the Northern Front nearly stopped, while hostilities continued on the Southwestern and Romanian fronts. The treaty's terms did not extend to Little Russia (Malorossiya) due to the partial Ukrainization of local authorities and the army. This circumstance arose because, on 26 June 1917, Prime Minister A.F. Kerensky of the Russian Provisional Government signed a protocol acknowledging the General Secretariat of the Ukrainian Central Council, which had taken on the role of the highest legislative body in autonomous Ukraine since April 1917.

Armored car units / Eastern Front 1918
An *Erhardt* M.1917 of the 4th Platoon registered to the *Armee-Abteilung B* operating in the West before the transfer to the Russian Front. (AC)

The 1st Armored Cars Detachment, comprising *Ehrhardt*, *Büssing*, and *Daimler* vehicles, on the Russian Front. The (**GG**-) prefix in the registration number indicates vehicles assigned to the Generalgouvernement Belgien (Civil Occupation Administration Belgium), suggesting that the photo was likely taken just after the transfer of armored cars from the Western to the Eastern Front. (AC)

Two *Ehrhardts* M.1917 in Ukraine (1918). The crew was photographed during a pause in combat. (AC)

Armored car units / Eastern Front 1918
An *Ehrhardt* M.1917 from the 3rd Platoon, with the individual tactical number 2 displayed on its bonnet, is seen entering Rostov-on-Don, August 1918. (NARA)

An *Ehrhardt* M.1917 of the 1st Detachment captured by the Red Army in the Kozinki area, Ukraine in May 1918. (AC) Note the interior view of the small combat compartment, designed to accommodate a crew of nine, protected by 9mm armor.

A colorized photo from March 1918 captures an *Ehrhardt* M.1915 vehicle from the 1st Detachment displaying the tactical markings *P.K.M.A.G.A. 1.* The vehicle's crew pauses briefly during a patrol near Mykolaiv, Ukraine. (NARA)

The Ukrainian People's Republic (UNR) proclamation occurred on 20 November 1917, with its independence officially confirmed on 22 January 1918. Faced with the threat of Soviet aggression, the Ukrainian Central Council sought military assistance from the Central Powers. The UNR delegation, still engaged in the Brest-Litovsk negotiations, reached a separate agreement with Germany and Austria. Responding to the Ukrainian plea for military aid, the German and Austro-Hungarian command mobilized their armies, pushing back Soviet forces. German troops swiftly recaptured a significant portion of Ukraine, including Kyiv, where the Central Council returned, and continued the offensive in Southern Russia.

The Imperial Army committed substantial forces to the Ukrainian operation, including scarce armored car units. On 19 February the German 1st Armored Car Detachment and the 2nd Platoon were transported by railway to Kovel and placed under the command of General Command Reserve 55 (*Generalkommando zur besonderen Verwendung Nr. 55 / Generalkommando z.b.V. Nr. 55*). In preparation for the upcoming German offensive, the 1st Detachment received reinforcements with new *Ehrhardts* M.1917, while the *Büssing* was assigned to the reserve. In the second half of February the armored car units advanced into Lutsk via Holoby, with the 2nd Platoon operating under the command of the 2nd Cavalry Division (*2. Kavallerie Div.*). Advancing eastward through Dubno, Rivne, Novgorod-Volynsky, and Zhytomyr, the German armored vehicles encountered no resistance along their route. On the morning of 5 March 1918 both the 1st Detachment and the 2nd Platoon successfully entered Kiev.

Following the signing of a peace treaty between Germany and the Ukrainian People's Republic (UNR), the activities of armored car units in Kyiv were primarily confined to policing functions. Despite the still relatively weak state of the Red Army, German mobile forces were reinforced.

In April the 4th and 5th Platoons were transferred to Ukraine from the Baltic States; on 3 May, the 3rd Platoon followed. In July newly-formed 7th and 8th Platoons were moved to the East, while the 6th Platoon remained stationed in Livonia. By early May 1918 all German combat-ready car armored units were present on the territory of the former Russian Empire. The main reason for the concentration of German motorized units was to prepare for an offensive against the Soviets.

While the Kyiv region was safeguarded by the 2nd Platoon, temporarily reinforced by the heavy and unreliable *Büssing* held in reserve, the 1st Detachment and the 3rd Platoon advanced south. From March to September these units operated along the line from Kyiv to Kharkiv, Rostov-on-Don, Mykolaiv, Crimea, and the Caucasus.

As of 17 March 1918 Austro-Hungarian and German forces successfully captured Nikolaev, initiating requisitions of food supplies and dismantling equipment from shipbuilding plants. On 20 March an uprising against the occupiers ensued, which was brutally suppressed within five days. During the fighting near the London Hotel, where General Command Reserve 52 (*Generalkommando z.b.V. 52*) was located, the Red Guards lost an *Austin III*, which went on to reinforce either the 1st Detachment or the 3rd Platoon.

The 1st Detachment, while continuing the advance on the Valuisky Front on 21 April, suffered significant losses in a battle near Kozinka (75 kilometers northeast of Kharkiv). German historians acknowledge the capture of one *Ehrhardt* M.1917 by the Red Army and the death of seven crew members. According to Soviet sources, confirmed by photographs, the Soviets also captured a second armored car, presumably the old *Ehrhardt* M.1915.

Armored car units / Eastern Front 1918
In the latter half of 1918, an *Ehrhardt* M.1917 from the 2nd Platoon, known as *Griep-to*, during recon missions in Ukraine. Note the disruptive camouflage composed of green, brown and yellow applied during the break in fighting during the summer. (AC)

Armored cars from the 2nd Platoon are seen being evacuated from Ukraine to Germany in September 1918. In the foreground is the *Büssing* (named *Grobetier*), with the *Ehrhardt* (named *Griepe-to*) following closely behind. Both vehicles are in three-color camouflage. (AC)

A photograph shows the *Büssing* vehicle in the barracks courtyard, likely at *Kraftfahrenkaserne* (Motorized Troops Barracks) in Wünsdorf close to Berlin, taken in September or October 1918. (AC)

Armoured car units. Western Front 1918
A photograph, most likely taken near Roubaix in France, captures an *Ehrhardt* M.1917 from the 3rd Platoon assigned to the *XVII.Armee,* formerly XIV. Army, which operated in Italy before being transferred to Flanders in the spring of 1918. (AC)

An *Ehrhardt* M.1917 of the 14th Platoon in 1918. (AC)

Initially assigned to the 1st Platoon, a captured French armored car *Peugeot* later served as a training vehicle in Wünsdorf Barracks before being reassigned to the 8th Platoon. This photo, taken in 1916, captures the vehicle shortly after its recovery from the battlefield near the village of Svystelnyky in Galicia. (AC)

By the end of May the 1st Detachment received reinforcement in the form of two captured *Austins*, and by June it reached Crimea. On 28 May the Menshevik government of Georgia was recognized by Germany, and agreements were signed in Poti, granting Germans exclusive rights to exploit Georgia's resources and placing the port of Poti and the railway under German command. Meanwhile, on 1 May 1918, German forces captured the town of Taganrog, and a few days later, they occupied Rostov-on-Don. The 3rd Platoon participated in that operation. The further advance was halted by the Red Army and workers' detachments, which attempted to organize a counterattack.

The Red Army command planned to use the newly formed 1st Extraordinary Division for a naval landing in Taganrog port with the aim of retaking the city. The landing was executed on 8-10 June at Miusliman between Taganrog and Zolotaya Kosa village. Approximately 6,400 Soviet soldiers with 12 guns established a bridgehead on the northern shore of the Mius Peninsula and, on 10-11 June launched an attack on Taganrog. The 3,000 Germans, supported by ten artillery batteries, two *Ehrhardts* of the 3rd Platoon, and several aircraft, put up fierce resistance. On the morning of 13 June the Germans circumvented the Soviets on their left flank, with an armored vehicle playing a crucial role in the breakthrough. By the evening, the encirclement of the landing force was completed, and only about 2,000 Red Army fighters managed to retreat onboard vessels of the Azov Flotilla. On the morning of 14 June German armored vehicles and cavalry conducted a clean-up of the battlefield.

On 3 August 1918 the 3rd Platoon entered Rostov-on-Don, but soon after, on 12 September, it was ordered to leave the territory of the former Russian Empire and relocate to France, where it remained until the war's end.

Meanwhile, on 1 August 1918, the 1st Detachment was transported by the Black Sea to the Georgian port of Poti. From there, they travelled by railway to Tbilisi, where the armoured cars became part of the Motorized Vehicles Column 801 (*Kraftwagen-Kolonne 801*), operating near the Georgian capital. The unit engaged in patrolling and guarding and awaited a planned raid on Baku, which ultimately did not take place. In early November the 1st Detachment returned to Poti, where it awaited evacuation from Georgia to Russia until mid-December. The Detachment eventually reached Nikolaev by ship on 17 December, a month after the Armistice, marking the effective end of the First World War for Germany.

The post-war evacuation of German forces from Russia posed significant challenges as Eastern Europe became increasingly unstable during the Russian Civil War. The traditional land transport routes through Poland were cut off, as the newly re-established country was at the edge of war with Germany. The railway routes to East Prussia were blocked by Ukrainians and Lithuanians. The 1st Detachment found itself trapped in the Nikolaev (nowadays Mykolaiv), which was taken over by Ukrainian Ataman N.A. Grigoriev, a supporter of Petliura. In December 1918 Grigoriev's insurgents even gained control of part of the Nikolaev, which was recaptured on 10 February 1919 by Greek troops.

The Beutepanzer Mark IV ('Fritz') of *Sturm-Panzer-Abteilung 14*, identified by the dark blue color of the cockade and the tactical number '5'. Tanks from the 1st and 11th Detachments used white markings; the 2nd and 12th used red; the 13th used yellow; and the 14th used blue. (Artwork by David Bocquelet)

A Beutepanzer Mark IV tank from an unidentified *Sturm-Panzer-Abteilung* in France, October 1918. On 7 July 1918, the Chief of the General Staff officially sanctioned the practice of covering armoured fighting vehicles with a multicolour scheme. It consisted of *Feldgrau*, *Lehmgelb* (two shades were possibly in use), *Rotbraun*, and *Grun* bands or stripes, outlined with two-finger wide lines painted *Schwarz*. The tanks is with the final variant of the *Balkenkreuz*, introduced in early October 1918. (Artwork by David Bocquelet)

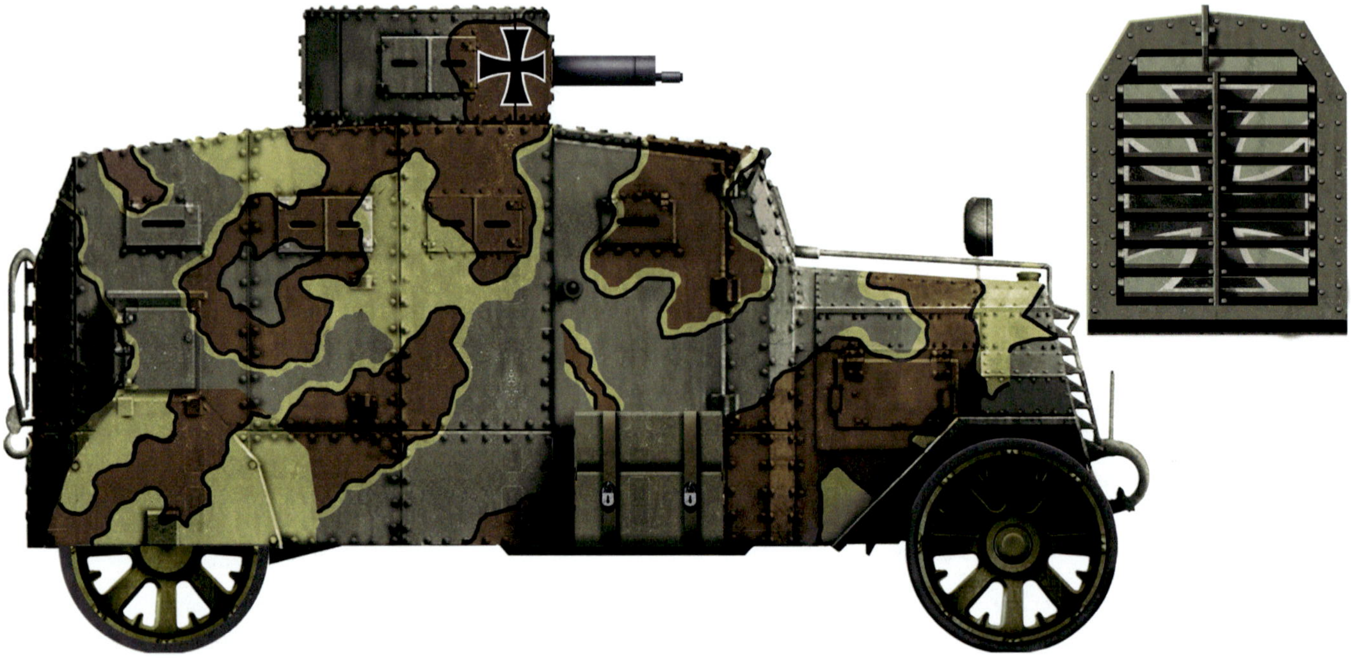

The Ehrhardt E-V/4 M.1917 of the 2nd Armoured Car Machine Gun Platoon (*Panzer Kraftwagen Maschinengewehr Zug* 2) Ukraine, Summer 1918. During the summer of 1918, the 2nd Platoon, tasked with policing functions in Kyiv, introduced camouflage to its combat vehicles, namely sevral Ehrhardt M.1917 and one Büssing A5P M.1915. Whether this initiative stemmed from grassroots efforts or was a response to the *Buntfarben Anstrich* (multicolour scheme) regulations issued by the *O.H.L.* in July 1918 remains unclear. (Artwork by David Bocquelet)

The Büssing M.1915 A5P, 'Grobetier', *Panzer Kraftwagen Maschinengewehr Zug 2*. Eastern Front / Ukraine, 1918. Operating this super-heavy armored vehicle in the vast and often rugged terrains of the Eastern Front presented significant challenges. The scarcity of paved roads and the difficult ground conditions—ranging from muddy fields to uneven, forested landscapes—severely limited its mobility and operational effectiveness. (Artwork by David Bocquelet)

A7V of the *Sturm-Panzer-Abteilung 1*, vehicle no. 5 (serial no. 562), which fell into a ditch on 9 June 1918 between Rollot and Courcelles-Épayelles on the Western Front. It bore a white cockade—identifying the 1st Assault Tank Detachment—and a skull with crossbones, the unit's individual emblem. (Artwork by David Bocquelet)

The A7V of the 2nd Assault Tank Detachment (*Sturm-Panzer-Abteilung 2*), vehicle No. III (serial No. 563), photographed in France, May 1918. Tanks of the 2nd Detachment were easily recognizable by their red Roman numeral tactical markings. During early combat missions, A7Vs were neither camouflaged nor named; however, over time, this tank was christened 'Wotan', drawing from folklore mythology—a practice that served both morale and propaganda purposes. (Artwork by David Bocquelet)

The towed 8.8cm cannon—primarily intended to engage high-flying reconnaissance aircraft and bombers—served with Motorized Heavy AAt batteries (*Kraftwagen-Schwere Flak-Batterien*) on the Western Front in 1918 A typical German heavy *Flak* battery was equipped with only two guns and a few K.D.I. 100 tractors.

An A7V Flakpanzer armed with two captured Russian 76mm guns, photographed in France in 1918. This self-propelled anti-aircraft platform was part of experimental efforts to increase mobile air defense for frontline units. It was painted in an experimental camouflage scheme of green-gray squares over an ochre background, designed to break up the vehicle's outline against varied terrain.

A 77mm Leichte Kraftwagengeschütze M.1914 of *A.O.K. 2 / K. Flak 36* (2nd Army Command, 36th Motorized Anti-Aircraft Detachment) in France, 1917. The vehicle is finished in a distinctive patchwork camouflage scheme, intended to blend into the varied terrain of the Western Front. This light motorized anti-aircraft gun provided mobile air defense against low and medium-flying enemy aircraft but was also used as a rapid reaction force against British tanks in emergency situations when they broke through the front line. (Artwork by David Bocquelet)

Armored car units / support vehicles
A mobile workshop from an identified motorized unit. Every armored car detachment included two trucks, one truck repair shop, and one staff car. (AC)

The auto workshop mounted on a NAG (*Neue Automobil Gesellschaft*) truck chassis of the 1st Armored Car Detachment. (AC)

A 1st Armored Car Detachment staff car was photographed somewhere in the East in 1918. Take note of the tactical markings painted on the bonnet (*P.K.M.G.A.1*).(AC)

Grigoriev later joined the Bolsheviks, and in March his Red brigade again captured Nikolaev and began disarming the remnants of the German troops. On 13 March, in the list of weapons handed over to Grigoriev by the Germans, two armored cars were listed, possibly the old *Daimler*, the *Ehrhardt* M.1917, or perhaps two *Austins*. It remains unclear whether the Germans handed over the cars to Grigoriev or simply abandoned or destroyed them themselves.

On 15-16 March 1919 the remaining German units in Nikolaev boarded ships under French command and were transported to Thessaloniki and interned there. In the summer of 1919, servicemen from the 1st Detachment, along with other German soldiers evacuated from Nikolaev, were brought back to Germany via the port of Emden.

Despite all the efforts, German armored car units played a minor role during the First World War. The total production, excluding makeshift, auxiliary, and experimental designs, amounted to only 15 vehicles (or 17 if semi-armored machine guns like the *Daimler* M.1914 are included). This figure does not contain a production order placed on 31 October 1917, for an additional two dozen *Ehrhardt* armored cars (M.1919), which became available only in 1919-1920, after the war had ended. Even with the addition of 20 to 30 captured armored cars in service, the German contribution remained significantly lower compared to the Allies, who employed nearly 1,000 armored cars by the war's end.

The Germans struggled not only with the limited production capacity but also failed to recognize the tactical value of armored vehicles early on. While they conducted experiments with armored cars from 1905 and incorporated them into military exercises, there was a notable shortcoming in perceiving their potential roles. When the war broke out, armored cars were still viewed primarily for patrolling or haulage purposes rather than combat. This perception began to shift only in 1915-16, which proved to be too late to establish armored vehicles as a prominent feature in German wartime armament.

The British tank attack at Cambrai
The British attack at Cambrai was launched on 20 November 1917. It was notable for being the first ever large-scale use of tanks in a coordinated assault. The British employed over 400 armored fighting vehicles, which surprised the German forces and achieved significant initial gains. However, the success was short-lived, as the British could not fully exploit their gains due to logistical and communication issues.
Following the German counter-attack at Cambrai, a destroyed British *Mark IV* tank and German soldiers in the village of Fontaine Notre Dame, located 4 kilometers west of Cambrai. Photo taken in November 1917. (AC)

A German captured *Mark IV* 'Male' tank (F.41, No.8019, Fray Bentos II) at the Cambrai railway station. F.41 was knocked out at Cambrai on 27 November 1917. (AC)

The British tank attack at Cambrai
After the Battle of Cambrai, the Germans salvaged many *Mark IV* tanks left behind by the British and repurposed them for their own use, incorporating them into their own armored forces.
A man from a *Sturm Bataillon* inspecting a damaged *Mark IV* (from the B / 2nd Battalion / Tank Corps, Serial no. 8052) that will soon be salvaged and incorporated into the German Captured Tank Detachment. (AC)

A *Mark IV* from the F / 6th Battalion / Tank Corps captured by the Germans in 1917. The letter indicated the battalion while the number identified individual tank (F.13). These numbers were generally located on the front horns and hull rear. (AC)

A Mark IV with burn-out tactical markings captured and guarded by the German soldiers. Note the missing tank corps marking, which consisted of white-red-white vertical stripes painted on the front horns of the tracks. (AC)

3
Assault Tank Detachments

3.1 Development of armored fighting vehicles

The challenges faced by the Imperial German Army in developing tanks during the First World War were a natural extension of their earlier struggles with armored cars. Just as the Germans had shown limited interest in armored vehicles before the war, their approach to tank development was also fraught with difficulties and delays. When the need for tanks became evident, the German military found itself ill-prepared to quickly develop and deploy these new machines.

The significance of tanks became evident to the Germans only during the British attack at Cambrai on 20 November 1917. On this day, the British armored fighting vehicles broke through German lines on a front of 12 kilometers to a depth of 9 kilometers, setting off a panic among some infantry units. Fortunately for the Germans, the *II.Armee* staged a counterattack in the sector on 29 November 1917 that erased the British salient and captured about 100 British tanks.

In the autumn of 1916, the *Kriegsministerium* gave orders to the *APK, GPK* and *VPK* to start to work, together with the German motor vehicle industry, on the first German assault armoured vehicle (*Sturmpanzerwagen*) known as *A7V*, a name coined by the Prussian War Ministry's A7V Section (*Abteilung 7 Verkehrswesen*), overseeing the project. A comprehensive specification covering both on and off-road performance, fully stowed weight, carrying capacity, armament, and engines was prepared. Oddly, the document lacked details on the thickness of the armor, possibly because a new armor-piercing bullet was undergoing testing, and the *A7V* committee might have been awaiting its findings.

Contracts with various component suppliers were initiated by mid-November 1916, even though the overall design, directed by Joseph Vollmer, the chief designer for the A7 Section, had not been finalized. By 22 December the Evaluation Commission for Transport Technology (*VPK*) approved the design and presented plans outlining the proposed general layout to the War Ministry.

On 1 February 1917 the *Kriegsministerium* specified an overall armor thickness of 30mm, leading to new plans. However, due to the weight of the armor reaching nine tonnes, the *A7V* Section decided to have 30mm armor only on the front, with the sides at 15mm and the rear at 20mm. Some tanks later received additional armor around the driver›s cabin sourced from mudguards. The *A7V* vehicle featured a box-like armoured structure mounted on running gear and tracks based on the American *Holt* agricultural tractor.

It was powered by a pair of Daimler four-cylinder, water-cooled petrol engines, each rated at 100hp, providing a total of 200hp—surpassing the British *Mark IV* in power.

Despite its superior suspension with sprung bogie wheels, the *A7V* had a limited ground clearance of only 20cm and struggled to cross gaps wider than approximately 2m. In terms of speed, it outperformed British tanks, reaching 10 to 14km/h on roads, nearly double the speed of a *Mark IV*. The *A7V* also carried more fuel (500 vs 315 liters) and had a slightly greater range than the *Mark IV*.

The *A7V* had a minimum crew of 18, which included a driver and commander. The driver was seated alongside the commander above the engines in the centrally situated ‹conning tower›; thus, his field of view was extremely restricted, particularly to the front. He had to contend with a blind spot extending some 15m to the front, which was extremely challenging, taking into account numerous shell holes 'on the battlefield way'. Other crew included two engineers – who were supposed to be able to fix a faulty engine and deal with other mechanical problems – a gunner and loader each to man six machine-gun positions around the hull plus a gunner and loader working the 5.7cm gun at the front of the tank. Sometimes a larger crew was carried, bringing the total up to 24 men. Not only could some of these men replace wounded members of the existing crew if required, but they were also carried to jump down and occupy captured trenches.

British tanks in German hands
A stripped *Mark IV* tank is being recovered by German troops in the aftermath of Cambrai. Two road locomotives and two sets of rollers, linked by chain, support the otherwise immobile tank. This is tank Serial No. 158, which caught fire in Bourlon village on 24 November 1917, and had to be abandoned. (AC)

German soldiers loaded a captured British *Mark IV* tank onto a railroad in November 1917. Photo taken close to Cambrai, France. (AC)

The German military tested captured British *Mark IV* tanks at several locations. One notable testing site was the *Krupp* proving grounds near Meppen, in northwestern Germany. Here, engineers and military personnel could examine the tanks in detail, assess their capabilities, and conduct trials to understand their design and operational strengths and weaknesses.
A *Mark IV* on the German testing ground, spring 1918. (AC)

Training (dummy) tanks
For tactical anti-tank training, the German Army deployed a series of *Holzpanzer* (wooden tanks), also known as *Panzerattrappen* (dummy tanks), starting in 1916. These replicas largely mimicked the British *Mark I-IV* models, characterized by their distinctive rhomboid shape. Mounted on carts or sleighs, they were typically towed by horses or soldiers, and only occasionally by motor vehicles (trucks). These dummy tanks were stationed at various training facilities in the rear areas behind the frontlines or on training grounds throughout Germany.
The crew of a mock-up *Mark I* tank quenched their thirst in a nearby Attigny Kantine while their machine attracted the attention of passers-by. (AC)

A wooden mock-up of an English 'Male' tank photographed somewhere in north-eastern France in September 1917. (AC)

The original plan included 'Male' (gun-equipped) and 'Female' (gun and machine gun-equipped) versions, but ultimately, 'Females' predominated. The chosen gun was a 5.7cm *Nordenfelt* captured from Belgian sources but originally British, which meant that it was very similar to the 5.7cm *Hotchkiss* gun in British tanks. Unfortunately there weren't enough of these weapons to arm each *A7V* with two, so the rear position was redesigned to accommodate two machine guns.

On the move, an *A7V* made a better gun platform due to its sprung suspension than the *British Mark IV*, which, if wanted to hit anything with its side-mounted guns, it was best to stop; otherwise, vibration made accurate shooting impossible.

The *A7V's* prototype was completed by *Daimler-Motoren-Gesellschaft* at Marienfelde plant near Berlin and tested on 30 April 1917. A wooden mockup of a final version was completed in May 1917 and demonstrated in Mainz with 10 tons of ballast to simulate the weight of the armour.

The first pre-production *A7V* was manufactured in September 1917, followed by the first production model in October 1917. During the acceptance tests, it was discovered that the engines were difficult to start and tended to overheat once they were running. There were also problems with tracks shedding and gearbox breakages. However, while such problems could be attended to, there was nothing that could be done about the *A7V's* major shortcoming – its poor obstacle-crossing ability – short of a complete redesign.

Although an initial order for 100 *A7V* chassis was placed in early 1917, only 20 of them were ultimately completed as combat vehicles. The remaining chassis were repurposed and converted into tracked cargo carriers, known as *A7V/U*.

While the Germans were concentrating on the introduction of *A7V* tanks, alternative designs were also in consideration. The *A7V-U*, standing for *Umlaufende Ketten* or 'tracks running all the way round,' was conceived as the successor to the *A7V*. It retained the Holt-type chassis but featured a rhomboidal hull and all-around tracks. Similar to British tanks, it housed 5.7cm main guns in sponsons on either side but maintained the high conning tower driver/commander station of the *A7V*.

Training (dummy) tanks
A large number of German soldiers took part in eight-day anti-tank courses, which were also attended by many soldier spectators. Machine guns and trench mortars fired against dummy tanks until they penetrated beyond the second line when the artillery took over the defense. Instruction was given in the vulnerable parts of the tank.
A unique dummy tank made of canvas. Was it a mock-up vehicle or a false target for enemy aviation or artillery? (AC)

Two wooden dummy tanks resembling *Mark Is* utilized for training purposes. Wooden models were produced in Ghent for training purposes from January 1917. (AC)

German tank prototypes
The *A7V* tank (No. 501, later named Gretchen) was one of the first to be produced, and it was undergoing testing at *Daimler Works* in late 1917. This particular *A7V* („Female' model) was equipped with MG 08 machine guns. It was initially painted in the standard *Feldgrau* (dark gray), but it was later given disruptive camouflage. (AC)

Above and top next page: In February 1918 tanks belonging to the 1st Armored Tank Detachment (*Sturm Pz.Abt.1*) were seen on the Doncourt training ground, engaging in exercises with *Sturmbataillion Nr 5* troops. These vehicles featured elongated front grilles and additional armor to simulate later weight configurations. Interestingly, the weight distribution was so well-balanced that the oversight of the 'low nose' error went unnoticed. Notably, no identification markings were visible on the tanks at this stage. (AC)

Sturm Pz. Abt. equipped with *A7V* tanks had a strength of 7 officers, 171 NCOs and men. The primary weapons of the first tank detachments were *A7V* armored fighting vehicles (5) plus passenger/staff cars (2), small truck (1), standard truck (1), mobile repair workshop truck (1), equipment truck (1) with trailer, 5 fuel supply trucks, one for each 5 trucks, one for each tank to supply of ammunition, spare parts, motorcycle (1) and trailer for field-kitchen (1).

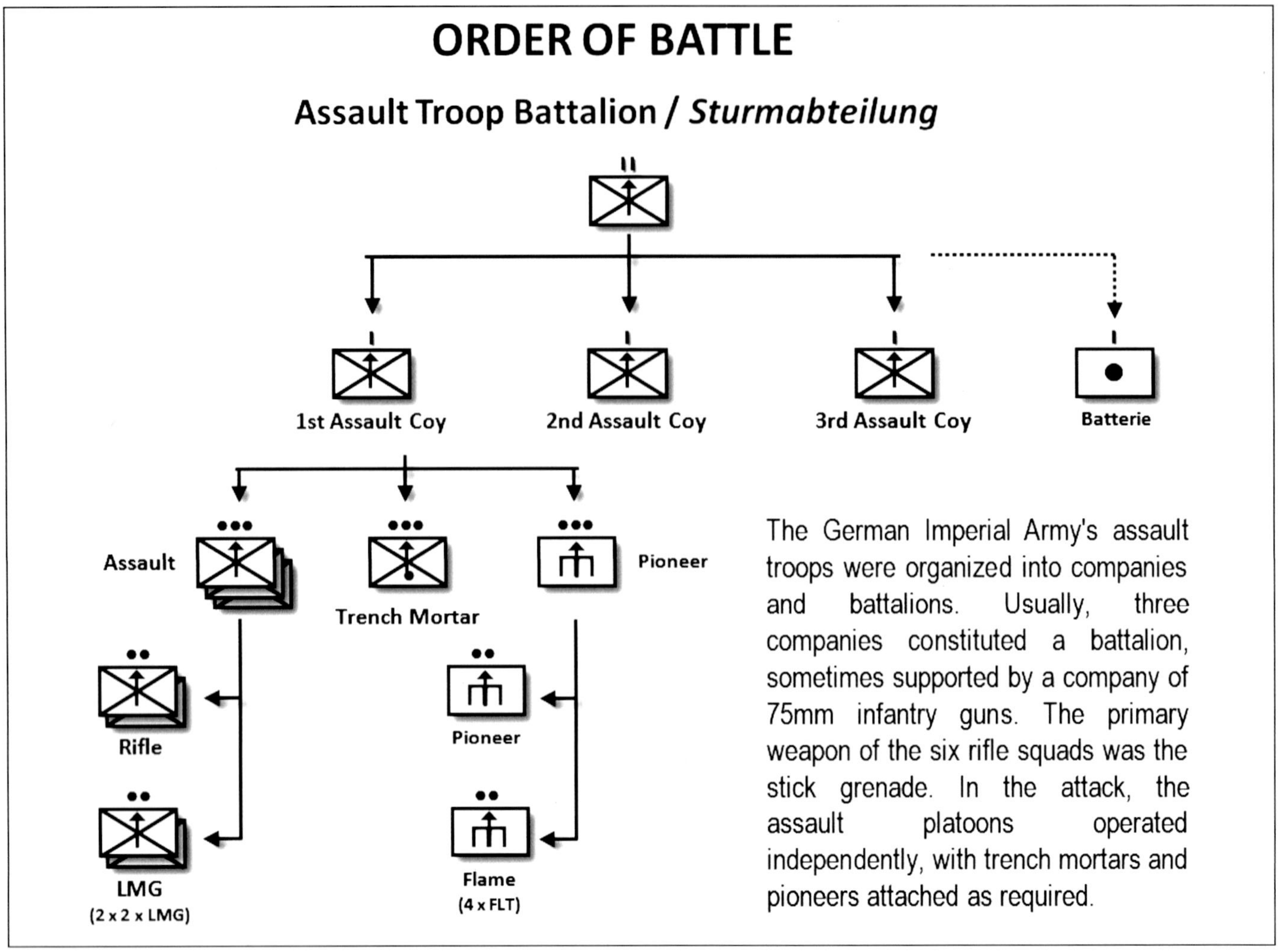

The German Imperial Army's assault troops were organized into companies and battalions. Usually, three companies constituted a battalion, sometimes supported by a company of 7.5cm infantry guns. The primary weapon of the six rifle squads was the stick grenade. In the attack, the assault platoons operated independently, with trench mortars and pioneers attached as required.

Assault Tank Detachments
Tanks from the 1st Detachments (501 and 506) undergoing repairs at the Bavarian Army Motor Vehicle Park 20 (*Bayerischer Armee-Kraftwagen-Park 20 / BAKP 20*) following the 21 March 1918 battle. The first vehicle bears a simple skull emblem on its bow (indicating it's a 'Female,, model equipped with a machine gun), whereas the second vehicle displays a skull with crossbones ('Male' tank armed with a gun). (Photo: Bayer Hauptstaatsarchiv / BH)

A7V tanks of the *Sturm Pz. Abt. 1,* marked with the death head symbol instead of the standard Iron Cross on their bow. The photograph was taken in France, near Rheims, during the summer of 1918. The number of vehicles in the picture suggests that this photo was taken at the staging area of three tank detachments. (AC)

An *A7V* of the 2nd Detachment goes to the front in the spring of 1918. (AC)

British Whippet Mark A tank in German service
Among the tanks captured by the Germans at Bray in March 1918 were two *Whippet Mark A's* (Serial Nos. A220 and A249). However, the commanding officer of the German Tank Force believed that the *Whippets* were the only Allied tanks worth copying; his opinion was ignored. With German new light tanks *LK II* already under construction, it was believed that enemy light tanks were not needed; thus, none of the captured *Whippets* were even put to use with the *Sturm Pz. Abt.*
A *Whippe*t (Serial No. A220) undergoing testing at *BAKP 20's* proving ground at Monceau-sur-Sambre. Photo taken in August 1918. The vehicle is probably in German multi-camouflage colours, with Iron Crosses applied. (IWM)

Bottom previous page and above: Following thorough testing, one of the *Whippets* was transported by rail to Berlin in November 1918. There, it was utilized by the *Freikorps* in January 1919 during clashes with leftist rebels. (AC)

A prototype of the *A7V-U*, a 40-ton tank, was constructed in June 1918, but trials revealed that it was excessively heavy and unwieldy. Additionally, the rails supporting the top run of the tracks tended to become clogged with earth, causing track displacement when the soil solidified. Despite the order for 20 production tanks in September 1918, none were assembled before the armistice took effect, leading to the discontinuation of the project.

In the spring of 1918, *Krupp* secured a contract to design a light tank (*leichte Kampfwagen*) and devised a design on 22 May. Following the French breakthrough at Villers-Cotterêts in mid-July 1918, utilizing their newly designed small Renault tanks, the German High Command (*OHL*) urgently called for the immediate mass production of *Krupps* armoured fighting vehicle. These were to be manufactured using components from passenger cars. Unfortunately, none of these new tanks were available before the end of the war.

3.2 Organization, training and tactical approach

While awaiting the introduction of new armored fighting vehicles, the formation of German tank detachments commenced. On 29 September 1917, following an agreement with the Chief of Field Motor Vehicles (*Chefkraft*), the Ministry of War issued orders to create Assault Tank Detachments Nos. 1 and 2 (*Sturm Panzer Kraftwagen Abteilungen 1* and *2*, abbreviated as *Stuka* or *Sturm Pz.Abt.*). The establishment of *Sturm Pz. Abt. 3* was ordered in December 1918. Each detachment comprised five *A7V* tanks, two passenger cars, one small and seven medium lorries, a field kitchen trailer, and a motorcycle. The leadership comprised one Captain, five subalterns, and 170 or 134 enlisted men. The staff roles included 81 drivers, 48 machine-gunners, 22 artillery personnel, 12 signalers, one medical orderly, and six supernumeraries. As already mentioned, the *A7V* crew size varied between 18 and 23 men, while crew members were drawn from various branches of services based on their skills.

The Imperial tank force was directly subordinated to the High Command (*OHL*), allocating scarce tank resources only for the most critical operations. Consequently, the Commander of the Combat Vehicle Detachments (*Kommand der Kampfwagenabteilungen*), responsible for all *Sturm Pz. Abteilungenkrafthahr* reported directly to the *OHL*, with the tank force generally considered part of the Motorized Troops.

The German industry's limited production capabilities and the shortage of *A7V* tanks were primarily supplemented by captured British tanks, specifically the *Mark IV*, referred to as *Beutepanzer*.

In December 1917 the *OHL* entrusted *Chefkraft* with the recovery and utilization of British tanks captured in the Cambrai area. The task was assigned to the Tank Recovery Command Cambrai (*Tankbergungsstelle Cambrai*), which was established from elements of *Armee-Kraftwagen-Park 2*.

New tank types under development
The *A7V's* potential successor, the *A7V-U* ('*U* for *umlaufende Ketten* or 'tracks running all the way round'), was unashamedly based on British tanks. It was still based on the Holt-type chassis but had a rhomboidal hull and all-around tracks. The main guns, 5.7cm again, were housed in sponson on either side, just like British tanks, but it retained the high conning tower driver / commander station of the *A7V*. The prototype was tested at Mainz on 25 June 1918. Twenty production tanks were ordered in September 1918, but none had been built by the time the armistice came into effect, so no more appeared. (Photo: Patton Museum / PM)

At the end of the War, Germany developed a light tank, the *Leichtkampfwagen LK I,* whose design proved unsuccessful during the trials in March 1918. (AC)

The improved *LK II*, armed with a 5.7cm gun, was designed in the summer of 1918 to take advantage of any breakthrough in the Allied trench lines. However, it came too late, never seeing action on the front. By December 1918 the firm *Steffen & Heymann* had assembled only 15 *LK IIs* in various stages of production. (AC)

Sturmabteilungen
The *Sturmbataillon Nr. 5* (Rohr) visited by the Kronprinz. Dated May 1917 in Doncourtwald. The 5th Battalion was chosen to assist the first German tank detachments on the battlefield. (AC)

Stormtroopers are inspected outside their rear billets before going into the lines, France, 1918. Note the characteristic steel helmets, the sandbags bulging with stick grenades and the puttees that have replaced the jackboots of 1914. (AC)

Stormtroopers clearing a trench, June 1918 (Marsoupes near Saint Michiel). Note a soldier who throws a grenade before the assault column rushes to reach the next part of the trench. They are equipped with a blanket, grenade bags, and the new steel helmet, but no rifle! Was the photo taken during exercises? (AC)

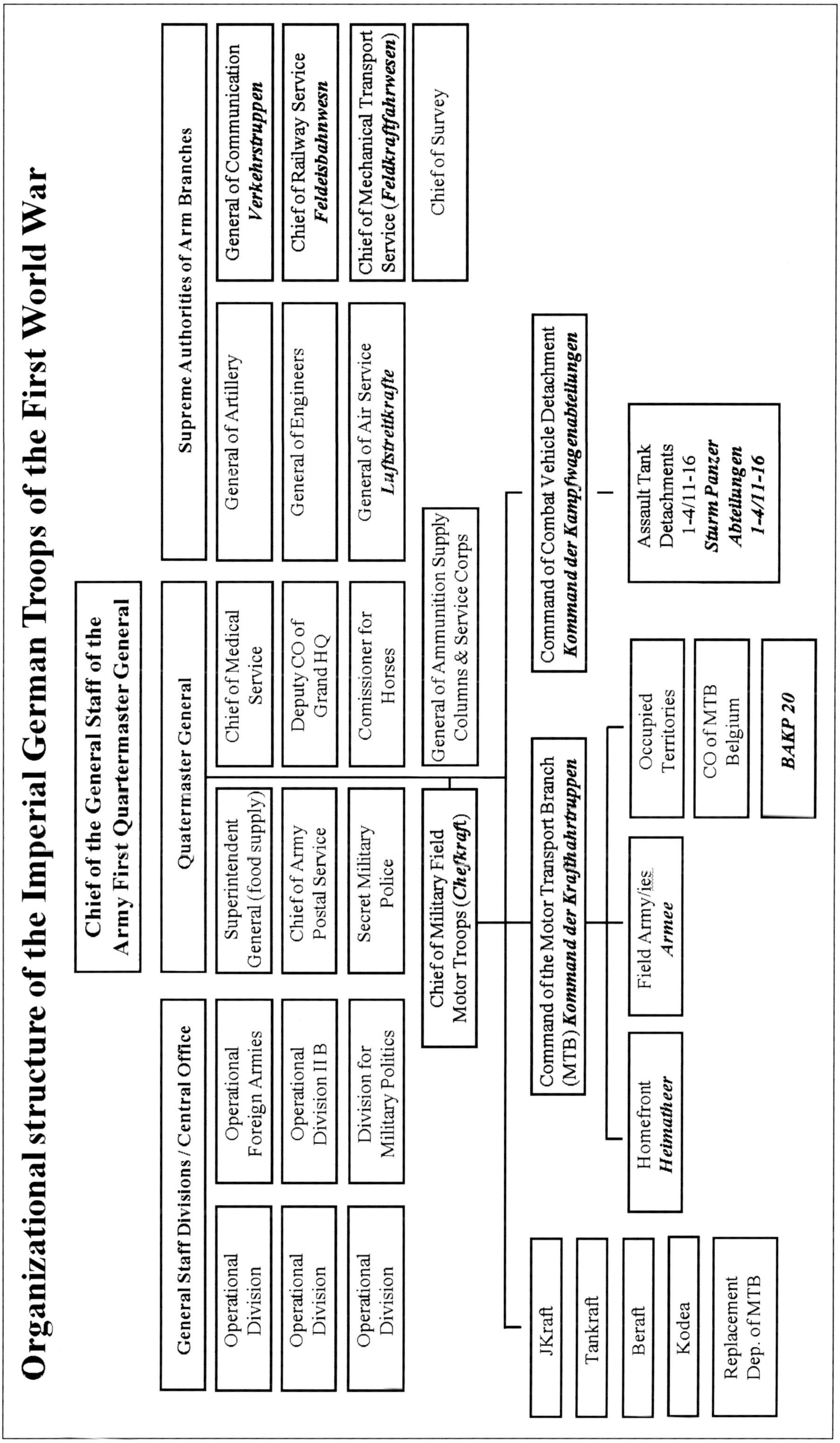

Organizational structure of the Imperial German Troops of the First World War.

1st Assault Tank Detachment
An *A7V* of the *Sturm. Pz. Abt, 1*; photo taken in June 1918 east of Reims. In mechanical terms, the *A7V* was a better tank than the British *Mark IV*, as it had a much more sophisticated transmission and a proper sprung suspension, albeit tucked under an armored shell and lacking the sort of profile suited to rough, uneven ground. (AC)

The *A7V* (Serial No. 560) of the 1st Detachment just after the Battle of Villers-Bretonneux on 24 April 1918. The German tank was basically a rectangular armoured box atop a modified *Holt* tractor chassis. The 32-ton vehicle was equipped with two *Daimler-Benz* four-cylinder, one-hundred-horsepower engines that generated a top speed of approx. 8,5km/h, so the vehicle was significantly underpowered for its weight and dimensions. (AC)

On 31 May 1918, the *A7V* (Serial No. 526) from the 1st Detachment moves forward to the assembly area. Leading the way is the tank commanded by Lieutenant Philipp, while Lieutenant Skopnik is outside, observing the road. (AC)

2nd Assault Tank Detachments

The *A7V*, christened Elfride from the 2nd Detachment, after its capture during the Battle of Villers-Bretonneux on 24 April 1918, displaying its Roman tactical number (III). Despite having 20mm steel plate at the sides, 30mm at the front and 10mm on the roof, the *A7V* was easily penetrated by cannon fire. This was because the steel was not a hardened armor plate and as such, it could only stop small-arms fire. (NARA)

The *A7V* (Serial No. 504, Tactical No: I, Name: Schnuck) of the 2nd Detachment on the move in May 1918. (AC)

On 31 August 1918 the 2nd Detachment suffered the loss of two tanks (528 and 504 Schnuck) at Fremicourt. In the photograph, the 528 (IV, Hagen), which got stuck, was abandoned and fell into the hands of the New Zealanders. (AC)

On 11 December 1917 the *OHL* ordered the establishment of a workshop for the assault tank detachments that were in the process of formation. For this purpose, the Bavarian Army Motor Vehicle Park 20 (*Bayerischer Armee-Kraftwagen-Park 20 / BAKP 20*) was made available. The town of Charleroi in Belgium was chosen as the location for the tank service center due to its excellent rail connections and workshop facilities taken after a Belgian railway-coach company.

The Tank Recovery Command Cambrai and *BAKP 20* worked diligently to restore as many captured tanks as possible, a challenging task given that many vehicles were damaged beyond repair. However, by the end of March they successfully restored 28 tanks, with 10 of them in working condition.

The operational *Mark IVs* were sufficient to equip two new tank detachments (number 11st and 12nd), each consisting of two 'Male' and three 'Female' vehicles. First *Beutepanzer* (Captured) *Sturm Pz. Abt. 11* became operational on 8 March 1918, followed by *Abt. 12* on 13 March. The next two *Beute Sturm Pz. Abts* were formed on 12 May (*Beute Sturm Pz. Abt. 13 Bavarian*) and 7 May (*Beute Sturm Pz. Abt. 14*), with two more formations in August (*Beute Sturm Pz. Abt. 15 & 16*).

In January 1918 the *A7V* made its field debut as the 1st Assault Tank Detachment, equipped with five *A7Vs,* arrived at the Bazeilles railway station on the eastern outskirts of Sedan. The new tanks were designated for the training of all tank crews, including those of 2nd and 3rd Detachments, both of which were still in the process of formation. Following a demonstration attended by the German Crown Prince, it was suggested to transfer the first tank detachment to Assault Battalion No. 5 (*Sturmbataillon Nr 5*) for a comprehensive six-week training program. Such an assignment was justified by the fact that the assault troops were formed to break the stalemate that artillery, massive wire entanglements and machine guns had imposed on conventional forces. These German 'sturm units' were so successful that assault companies were attached to many infantry divisions in the front line. By 1918, a total of 18 fully-fledged assault battalions had been established and integrated into German armies. Each battalion included essential elements such as light artillery, machine guns, trench mortars, and flame-throwers, in addition to infantry assault companies, demonstrating the evolving nature of military tactics.

The initial training of tank crews assumed that the armored fighting vehicles would be operating as a supporting arm akin to a heavily protected mobile gun, often lacking cooperation with infantry on the battlefield, typical for armored car platoons. The tactical disparities between tanks (off-road mobile fortresses) and armored cars (on-road reconnaissance vehicles) stemmed not only from technical design differences or fundamentally distinct abilities to overcome terrain obstacles but also from their subordination to different branches of arms and sections of the *Kriegsministerium* (Armored cars - A2 Section (Infantry) vs Tanks - A7 Section (Motorized Troops/Heavy Guns)).

Armoured car units functioned as part of the *Machinegewehrtruppe* or machine gun units, operating under the Guard Corps Substitute Command (*Stellvertretende Generalkommando des Garde Korps*). Personnel for this formation were primarily recruited from machine gun squads, supported by volunteers from motorized troops (*Kraftfahrtruppe*) and signal service. The tank force's development began under the supervision of artillerymen managing the armoured department established at the High Command (*OHL*), resulting in mobile fortress tactics.

2nd Assault Tank Detachment
'Female' (MG equipped) tanks of the *Sturm Pz. Abt. 2* (Serial Nos/Tactical Nos/Names: 504, I, Schnuck / 563, III, Wotan / 525, II, Siegfried) wait for entraining—photo taken in July 1918. (BK / AC)

An *A7V* of the *Abt.2* (Serial No. 525, Name: Siegfried) and his crew after the battle at Villers-Bretonneux on 24 April 1918. With the help of another *A7V*, Siegfried spoiled the attack of seven British *Whippets* east of Cachy. (NARA)

The *A7V* (563, Wotan) of the *Sturm Pz. Abt.2* was painted a solid *Feldgrau* but covered with dust. Note the large, red Roman tactical number (III). An *A7V* crew consisted of 17 soldiers and one officer. These were needed for the following roles: commander, driver, mechanic, two artillerymen (gunner and loader) and 12 infantrymen (six gunners and six loaders). (NARA)

Assault Tank Detachments
In the early summer of 1918, the 2nd Detachment participated in a demonstration some 40km east of Villers-Bretonneux, while *A7Vs* Nos. 502/540, 505 and 507 underwent transition to Sockellafette mounts at the nearby workshop. The closest vehicle is likely to be No. 503 (with removed front rear conn plates), with Nos. 505 or 507 in the middle (before the change) and 504 in the distance. (NARA)

A7V suspension view which was equipped with helical springs, rear-drive sprockets, front-mounted idlers and 24 roller wheels in bogies. The lack of shock absorbers made the ride incredibly bumpy, and the low clearance (190-400mm) led to poor off-road capabilities. (AC)

A7V (503) of *Sturm Pz. Abt. 3.* Tinkelberg training ground near Saarburg. Photo taken between late August and early September 1918. (Alamy)

The effective use of such tactics was hindered by the limited off-road performance of early tanks, necessitating thorough terrain surveys and reconnaissance before action. Tanks faced limitations such as the inability to mount walls over 1.5 meters high, susceptibility to halting in ditches or dense obstacles, and challenges in navigating mud, swampy ground, or soft sand. The *A7Vs*, weighing around 33 tons when combat-loaded, exhibited poor speed, maneuverability, and obstacle negotiation due to being underpowered and poorly balanced, achieving a top cross-country speed of 8.5km/h with a range of about 32 kilometers.

Tactical constraints also arose from challenging crew working conditions. Tank crews endured extreme heat, loud engine and running gear noise, dizzying fumes, cramped spaces, violent movements during cross-country travel, poor visibility, and constant fire hazards. Specific roles within the crew faced additional challenges, such as the loader dealing with limited space, heavy ammunition, and dangerous gun recoil, the gunner managing target acquisition and gun operation, and the commander multitasking navigation, route determination, target searching, formation maintenance, and crew coordination.

3.3 Tanks in action

The inaugural combat of German tanks took place near St. Quentin on 21 March 1918. At that time, only two detachments were ready: *Sturm Pz. Abt. 1* (5 x *A7V*) and *Sturm Pz. Abt. 11* (5 x *Mark IV* 'Females'). These tanks were assigned to assault troops from *Sturmbataillon Nr. 5,* serving as the vanguard for the *36th Inf. Div.* Among the five tanks of the 1st Assault Tank Detachment, three experienced mechanical breakdowns either before or during their entry into combat. Nevertheless, the remaining two tanks have played a role in repelling a minor British breakthrough, reaching their objective, and thus accomplishing their mission successfully. Despite revealing limited cross-country capability during this initial operation, *A7V* tanks demonstrated notable advantages, including potent firepower, enhanced mobility, sufficient protection, and the ability to accompany assault troops on relatively favourable terrain.

The former British tanks of *Sturm. Pz. Abt. 11* were less successful. Initially, they managed to keep pace with the infantry, but with improved visibility, the infantry quickly outpaced them, leaving the tanks to follow at a slower pace. The original objective of the detachment, to lead the assault, remained unaccomplished, and two tanks were damaged by shell fire while suppressing enemy trenches and machine gun nests.

On 9 April 1918 the German tanks were tasked with supporting Operation Michael near the marshy areas alongside the River Lys. However, the *A7Vs* encountered difficulties on rough terrain. The attempt by the captured tanks of *Sturm Pz. Abt. 11* and *12* turned into a fiasco, with nearly all the tanks breaking down or getting stuck in the soft soil.

On 24 April 1918 *Sturm Pz. Abt. 1-3,* equipped with *A7Vs*, with the *II.Armee* units, took part in an assault on the village of Villers-Bretonneux, the forest Bois d'Aquenne located southwest of it, and the village of Cachy, defended by British infantry. The battlefield was shrouded in heavy fog, severely hindering orientation. Group I, composed of three tanks, had a clearly marked area of attack, bounded by the railway line to the south and the Roman Road. Group II experienced a breakdown, starting with only six tanks. Group III formed two echelons: a northern one with two tanks supporting the *Inf.Regt. 419* and a southern one with two tanks supporting the *Inf.Regt. 257.*

Assault Tank Detachments
The photograph shows *A7V* tanks (Nos and names: 505, Baden; 507, Cyklop; 501, Gretchen) with their crews in France, Harbonnieres, August 1918. (NARA)

Two *A7V* tanks moving through a village, probably during a training session near Rheims in June 1918. The tanks in the photograph are probably (Serial No. 504, Name: Schnuck) to the left and (Serial No. 528, Name: Hagen) to the right. According to the information provided, Hagen was lost at Fremicourt during the summer of 1918. The *A7V* was armed with a front 5.7cm *Maxim-Nordenfelt* main gun along with at least six 7.92mm Maxim MG 08 machine guns in flexible mounts along the flanks and rear. (NARA)

Two *A7V* tanks of *Sturm Pz. Abt. 2* marked with distinctive Roman tactical numbers (II and III). The front vehicle is stuck in a ditch, while the second is attempting to recover it. The 30-ton *A7V*, could be moved only with the help of another tank or a team of two heavy artillery tractors. (AC)

Assault Tank Detachments
This captured *A7V* (Serial No. 544, Tactical No. I, Name: Schnuck) was taken by the British soldiers at Bapaume, France, probably in December 1918. This is a side view of the tank, showing the spring bogies that were used for the tracks. The tank is painted in disruptive camouflage with a Roman numeral tactical number in red and a white outline, which indicates that it belonged to the 2nd Detachment. (IWM)

An *A7V* and ex-British *Mark IV* tanks on railway flatbeds. The *A7V* has its cupola removed to enable it to pass underneath rail bridges, which was a common practice to transport tanks by railway. Note the Iron Cross on the front plate of *Mark IV*, 'Female' type. (NARA)

A7V tanks of the *Sturm Pz. Abt. 1*, No. 540 and probably No. 560 following behind, shortly after the Battle of la Montagne de Reims against the French on 15 July 1918. At the time, No. 540 had a white ring with an individual tactical number (5), which can just be discerned in the photo. (AC)

Initially, the Germans successfully captured Villers-Bretonneux, with the tanks penetrating the Allied frontline and creating a 5-kilometre gap. During this operation, *A7Vs* engaged British tanks in the first tank versus tank battle in history. During a counterattack, three *A7V* tanks damaged two British *Mark IV* 'Female' tanks from the 1st Tank Battalion. In a subsequent engagement, a male *Mark IV* tank damaged the leading *A7V*, prompting a German retreat. Later in the day, another tank versus tank skirmish occurred when seven British *Whippet* tanks attacked the German *77th Reserve Div.* The *Whippets* were ambushed from two sides by 7.7cm field guns and several *A7Vs*. German fire knocked out four *Whippets* and disabled the *Mark IV*. The attack on Villers-Bretonneux marked a significant success for the German tank force, aided by the favourable terrain and the fog. However, the Imperial High Command barely acknowledged the attack, as Australian forces reclaimed most of the salient in a counterattack a few days later.

Towards the end of May (27-28), six assault tank detachments (Nos.*1-3, 11-13*) were deployed to support an assault against the French 6th Army in the direction of the Marne. The objective was straightforward: advance towards Reims and overcome all enemy resistance. Once again, the *Mark IVs* proved too slow for a swift infantry advance, and *Abt.12* demonstrated that the *Beutepanzers* needed greater strength and less clumsiness to quell determined enemy resistance. Once spotted by enemy artillery, these slow monsters had no means of escape. None of the tanks could traverse a wide trench in the French line known as the Dardanelles Trench. The only recourse was a retreat, leaving many vehicles in an unserviceable state, unfit for further action.

A few days later, on 31 May, *Sturm Pz. Abt. 2* entered combat near Pierquin Ferme north of Reims and prematurely lost two tanks due to technical breakdowns. Out of the remaining three machines, the lead tank was heavily damaged by French artillery and ultimately destroyed. The two remaining tanks turned back.

On 1 June 1918 *Sturm Pz. Abt. 1, 13,* and *14* (5 x *A7V* and 10 x *Mark IV*) supported the *238th Inf. Div.* launched an attack northwest of Fort de la Pompelle, west of Rheims, with the objective of securing the north bank of the Marne Canal. Prior to the combat, two *A7Vs* from the 1st Assault Tank Detachment experienced breakdowns. Upon reaching the French trench line, two of the three remaining *A7Vs* became stuck, and the attack was called off. The assault by *Sturm Pz. Abt. 13* and *14,* equipped with *Mark IVs*, faced initial setbacks. Two tanks broke down before reaching the start line, and a third retreated to German lines due to mechanical issues. Although two other *Mark IV* tanks played a useful role in the fighting around Fort de la Pompelle, both were ultimately lost in action. Interestingly, the *Beutepanzer* attack demonstrated that even *Mark IVs* could achieve some results, given limited objectives and the absence of readily available enemy field guns. Had *Abts 11* to *14* not been recklessly expended on 27 May, the combined force of 20 vehicles might have successfully secured victory at Fort de la Pompelle.

The losses on 31 May and 1 June necessitated the redistribution of tanks. The 1st Assault Tank Detachment, having lost two machines and with another undergoing extensive repairs, received two refurbished tanks, bringing their strength to four machines.

Villers-Bretonneux Battle

A7V (Name: Elfride) of the *Sturm Pz. Abt. 2* after its capture during the Battle of Villers-Bretonneux on 24 April 1918, displaying its name and Roman tactical number (III). Did she accidentally fail, or did the six-pounder British gun of a *Mark IV* force her out of action … or both? (BK)

Elfride (Tactical No. III) was salvaged and restored to an operational condition in Saleux on 25 May 1918. The British and French shared a victory celebration over Germany's new weapons and conducted basic field tests. (IWM)
Like many other military vehicles from the Great War, captured *A7Vs* were eventually scrapped. The high cost of maintaining and storing these large machines, combined with the lack of immediate use for them, led to their dismantling. Metal parts were often recycled, and other components were discarded or repurposed. (AC)

An *A7V* tank entrained at the station of Amagne-Lucquy in Northern France in May 1918. The vehicle is in plain field gray colour and carries Iron Cross markings. (AC)

An unidentified *A7V* from the 2nd Detachment during field exercises in the second half of 1918. The *A7V's* power came from two centrally mounted *Daimler* four-cylinder petrol engines, each capable of generating 100hp. At full power, the *A7V* could travel at a maximum speed of 15km/h. (AC)

The *A7V* (No. 505). Note the white serial number painted on the inside of the side hatch. (AC)

By the end of June the prospects for the *Beutepanzer* units were more promising than those of the *A7V* units, as a few hundred damaged British tanks were behind German lines, with about 40 of them mostly intact.

By 30 June the recovery teams from *BAKP 20* successfully relocated 85 British tanks to the Charleroi workshop and salvaged parts from another 48 tanks. In early August 1918, *Chefkraft* estimated that up to 170 captured British tanks could be restored, surpassing the technical capacity of *BAKP 20*. With the substantial number of captured tanks available and the cessation of *A7V* production, the Ministry of War decided to disband the nascent *Sturm Pz. Abt. 4* through *7*. Their crews were then reassigned to reinforce captured tank units.

During the summer, two new *Beutepanzer* detachments were established, namely *Sturm Pz. Abt. 13* and *15*, with plans for an additional seven. However, by the war's conclusion, there were only enough tanks and personnel for seven captured tank units, specifically *Sturm Pz. Abt. 11* to *16*.

As of 7 July 1918 the German Army had a total of eight assault tank detachment either in the field or undergoing training, each equipped with five tanks. However, only three of these units were equipped with German *A7V* tanks, while the remaining five utilized captured British *Mark IVs*.

The German attempts to isolate Reims had proven unsuccessful for the time being, and the city continued to pose a challenge to the German front line. On 9 July the German *XVIII.Armee* launched an offensive against the French salient along the River Matz. All available *A7V* units, totaling seven tanks, were allocated to this operation, but two of them broke down during the preparatory phase. As the attack commenced, the 3rd Assault Tank Detachment equipped with five *A7V* tanks provided the sole support and was divided between two infantry divisions. Although the tanks advanced behind the front elements of the infantry in favourable terrain, they achieved little and were non-operational and in dire need of repair by the end of the day.

In July preparations were underway for a new German offensive, where all assault tank detachments were to be deployed. *Abts 11* to *14* were assigned to support the *III.Armee* east of Reims and *Abts 1* to *3* were to operate with the *VII.Armee*; however, the serviceability of tanks was low.

On 15 July at 0450 hours, the attack commenced with the use of twenty *Beutepanzers* in the Reims sector of the French front during the Second Battle of the Marne. The captured *Mark IV* tanks from *Sturm Pz. Abts 11-14* performed well in the initial phase, advancing toward Souain and, in most cases, reaching and overcoming the first French defensive line. However, the French, adopting the German anti-tank practice, maintained the first trench line with minimal strength, contributing to the ease of the German advance. Once beyond the initial trench line, the German tanks encountered the heart of the French defenses, with several breaking down or getting trapped in trenches and eight being disabled by field guns.

The Souain attack resulted in significant losses for the captured tank units, and the combat contribution of the tanks proved to be minimal. Unlike the *Mark IVs*, the *A7Vs* showcased their advantages. Immune to small arms fire, they accelerated the infantry assault but did not accomplish anything beyond the capabilities of the infantry, given another hour or two to achieve their objectives. The Souain attack marked a turning point on the Western Front, signaling the German Army's shift to a defensive stance. The German offensive was halted just as a significant Allied counteroffensive commenced on the same day. Three days later, the Allies crossed the Marne, prompting the Germans to retreat to their former Aisne-Vesle lines.

German tanks stuck in action
A7V tanks frequently became stuck in wide trenches and shell holes despite their superior suspension with sprung bogie wheels, but with a limited ground clearance of only 20cm, making it challenging to traverse gaps wider than approximately 2 meters. The driver, positioned above the engines in the centrally located 'conning tower,' had an extremely restricted field of view, especially to the front. Consequently, he had to contend with a blind spot extending some 15 meters ahead, which posed significant challenges, particularly considering the numerous shell holes littering the battlefield. (AC)

Bautepanzer in action
After the Battle of Cambrai in late 1917, the Germans captured a large number of knocked-out and abandoned British tanks, particularly the *Mark IV*. These tanks were then repaired, rebuilt, and put into service by the German army under the designation *'Schwerer Kampfwagen (Beute)'* (Heavy Combat Vehicle (Captured)), in short *Bautepanzer*. (NARA)
The photograph shows the repaired by the Germans *Mark IV* tank. The overhaul was carried out at the Societé Anonyme Saint Germain plant in Monceau-sur-Sambre (Charleroi, Belgium) by the *BAKP 20* personnel. The battle-ready tanks were loaded onto a railway platform for transport close to the front lines. (NARA)

A re-marked ex-British *Mark IV* 'Female' tank on the advance to the front in Armentieres, France, in 1918. (IWM)

A *Beutepanzer Mark IV*, likely from *Sturm Pz. Abt. 11*, during military exercises near Essen, Germany, probably at the beginning of September 1918. During this period, ex-British tanks were intensively used to familiarize the Imperial German infantry with their sight and to learn how to fight them. (NARA)

In mid-summer 1918, the German tank force faced the need for reassessment and reconstruction. The heavy losses of *Beutepanzers* required a new set of tanks to re-equip *Abts 11-14* and form two new *Abts 15* and *16*. The decline in *A7V* numbers below the five-tank strength for the three *A7V* units, coupled with a shortage of spare parts, led the Charleroi workshop to dismantle two tanks for parts to repair others. Despite these efforts, by the end of June *Sturm Pz. Abt. 1* and *2* were reduced to four tanks each, and *Sturm Pz. Abt. 3* had only two.

By the end of July the Allies initiated counterattacks. The defensive posture of the German Army during the summer did not favor the use of tanks, but in late August, a limited counteroffensive was planned in the Cambrai area. Before eventually retreating to the 'Siegfried' position (commonly known as the 'Hindenburg Line' by the British), the German *II, XVII,* and *XVIII Armies* assumed an intermediate position during the night of 26/27 August.

On 31 August the 2nd and 3rd Assault Tank Detachments were assigned to support a counterattack near Fremicourt. *Sturm Pz. Abt. 1* failed to reach the combat area in time, resulting in the failure of the advancing infantry division›s attack. *Sturm Pz. Abt. 2*, with three of its four tanks, launched the attack, but the Bavarian infantry, unaware of tank support, did not advance with them. After a brief engagement with New Zealand troops, *Sturm Pz. Abt. 2* returned to the German lines. Unfortunately, German artillery, unaware of their identity, damaged two tanks and knocked out a third. This incident, deemed shameful and reported at the highest level, discouraged army commands from seeking tank support in the following months. Following the Fremicourt disaster, *Sturm Pz. Abt. 2* was effectively disbanded by being subordinated to *Sturm Pz. Abt. 1*.

At this stage, the *A7V* units awaited orders behind the Siegfried defensive line. With no further offensive operations anticipated, the High Command (*OHL*) considered alternative uses for the tank units, comprising 12 *A7V* tanks and 36 *Mark IV* tanks in nine detachments. Recognizing the ineffectiveness of the small units, plans were made to consolidate all *A7Vs* into a battalion-sized formation.

While stationed behind the frontline, the German tank units spent much of the early fall engaged in anti-tank training to acclimate the German infantry to the presence of armoured fighting vehicles. This training became crucial as tank panic spread in some Imperial units, posing a significant problem exacerbated by the increasing presence of Allied tanks.

By the end of September 1918 the Allies were approaching the Siegfried Line and prepared to breach it. In this situation, the *OHL*, on 24 September 1918, directed all nine tank detachments to concentrate in the area behind Army Group-German Crown Prince. The purpose was to act as a mobile strategic reserve, ready to repulse any major Allied offensive. With twelve *A7Vs* and approximately thirty-six *Mark IVs*, there was potential for significant impact. The number of *Mark IVs* was bolstered as most reserve tanks were transferred to frontline detachments.

This plan was short-lived, and instead, only one *A7V* unit (*Abt. 1*) and four captured tank detachments (*Abts 11, 13, 15, 16*) were transferred to the *XVII. Armee*, while *Abts 3, 12*, and *14* were to remain with their respective army groups and continue anti-tank training.

Bautepanzer in action
Training ground for assault troops near Rethel in 1918. Possibly a Field Combat School (*Feldkriegsschule)* of an unidentified *Armee Oberkommando.* Combat schools were established to train storm battalions capable of destroying machine gun nests, bunkers and armored fighting vehicles. (AC)

A 'dramatic' view of a complete detachment of *Baupenpanzer* tanks during a training exercise in the summer 1918. (AC)

A captured *Mark IV* tank from an unidentified detachment, damaged in action, undergoes inspection by interested German troops. (AC)

Bautepanzer in action
Ex-British tanks in German service often suffered from mechanical failures, which limited their operational capabilities. Additionally, due to their slow speed, they often had trouble keeping up with the fast-moving infantry during battles, which further hindered their effectiveness in combat.
This photograph shows German soldiers standing on top of a *Mark IV* tank, which they have named Hanni, in July 1918. (AC)

A captured British tank maintained and resupplied by its German crew. The location and exact unit of the tank are not specified. Note large German Iron Cross emblems painted on vehicle sides that help to differentiate between the friend or foe *Mark IVs.* (NARA)

A *Mark IV* tank of the *Sturm Pz. Abt. 13* (Bavarian) with a blue ring (cockade) and the individual tactical number (2) painted on it. (AC)

Meanwhile, on 22 September 1918, the Prussian Ministry of War ordered the name of the tank detachments to be changed from *Sturm Panzer Kraftwagen Abteilung* to *Schwere* (Heavy) *Kampfwagen Abteilung*. However, until 30 November 1918, both names were permitted for use in official correspondence.

By late September *Sturm Pz. Abt. 1* and *2* were reduced to only six *A7Vs*, so, as mentioned earlier, they were consolidated under the command of *Sturm Pz. Abt. 1*. To bolster the defense against an anticipated Allied breakthrough near Cambrai, the unit was relocated near the city in early October.

On 7 October 1918 the 3rd Assault Tank Detachment participated in a counterattack of the *III. Armee* at St. Etienne. All its tanks sustained damage during the battle, forcing the attack to be abandoned as the bridges over the Arne had already been blown up. The unit was ordered back to the Charleroi workshop for repair. Upon arrival at Charleroi, there was limited opportunity to repair and maintain the vehicles as the workshop was already being dismantled. On 21 October *BAKP 20* was evacuated to the Wiesbaden-Mainz area in Germany, and it is believed that *Sturm Pz. Abt. 3* joined this transport.

On 8 October 1918 *Sturm Pz. Abt. 15* was tasked with supporting an infantry counterattack near Maison Neuve. The Germans launched vigorous counterattacks, backed by tanks, to halt the Allied offensive on a 27km front south of Cambrai. While approaching the town, *Sturm Pz. Abt. 15* encountered British tanks of A Company, 12th Tank Battalion. There was considerable confusion on both sides, with the Germans thinking the tanks might belong to the neighboring *Sturm Pz. Abt. 16*, while the British suspected they might be from neighboring C Company. Both sides finally realized their identity when they closed to about 50m, and a fierce gunfight ensued. The German gun-armed tanks quickly knocked out one of the British machines with two simultaneous hits from their 5.7cm guns, while 12.7mm rounds disabled three more British tanks. As a confused melee broke out on the slopes east of the village, the British infantry began to withdraw back through Niergnes. In a somewhat ironic turn of events, British infantry brought an abandoned German field gun back into action against their former owners. One of the *Beutepanzers* was destroyed by this gunfire, and the remaining three withdrew. The German tank attack halted the British infantry advance and managed to disable four British tanks for a loss of four of their own, resulting in a drawn match. By the end of the day, neither *Sturm Pz. Abt. 15* nor A Company, 12th Tank Battalion, had no operational tanks.

The neighboring *Sturm Pz. Abt. 16* had even less success while supporting a German infantry counterattack near Seranvillers. Its three tanks encountered a British infantry column supported by tanks of C Company, 12th Tank Battalion. The fourth German, *Mark IV* did not encounter any British tanks and spent its time engaging British infantry positions around Seranvillers. The following day, both *Sturm Pz. Abt. 15* and *16* were directed back to Charleroi with the surviving seven Mark IV tanks, but three were left behind after breaking down.

A few days later, on 11 October, British infantry broke through German lines near Iwuy and Rieux, northeast of Cambrai. *Sturm Pz. Abt. 1*, with *A7Vs*, and *Sturm Pz. Abt. 13*, with three *Mark IVs*, were ordered to counterattack in support of German infantry. *Sturm Pz. Abt. 13* failed to reach the start line after losing two tanks to mechanical problems, while *Sturm Pz. Abt. 1* attacked the advancing British troops, causing them to quickly fall back. On the way back, one of the *A7Vs* was targeted by enemy artillery, heavily shelled, and, no longer serviceable, abandoned.

Beutepanzer in action
A tank of the *Sturm. Pz. Abt. 12* near Pontavert in May 1918. The German tank force was used during the (Third) Battle of the Aisne against a minor and tired British force, which was struck and virtually destroyed. (AC)

A tank of the *Sturm Pz. Abt. 12* bogged down near Fromelles on 9 April 1918. Note the early camouflage, which consisted of red-brown and mud-yellow patches on *Feldgrau.* (BH)

Beutepanzer Mark IV (110) of the *Sturm Pz. Abt.12.* The photo is dated 27 May 1918. Note the red rings and black Iron Crosses painted on the sides and back of both tanks. (AC)

Beutepanzer in action
A glimpse of a *Beutepanzer*, likely from *Sturm Pz. Abt. 12*, left abandoned somewhere on the Western Front during the summer of 1918. (AC)

A *Mark IV* from *Sturm Pz. Abt. 12* (Tactical No.5, Serial No. 107) lost during the fighting near Fort de la Pompelle (Front de Champagne) on 1 June 1918. The crew dismounted from its tank to assist the infantry in resisting a French infantry attack. Note red cockades identifying the 2nd Detachment and black Iron Crosses. Note that the tactical number (5) had a slightly different typeface on each side. (AC)

All other tanks of the 1st Assault Tank Detachment (reinforced) safely returned to the Charleroi workshop. Given the urgency, there was no time for repairs, and the worn-out tanks were transported to Wiesbaden-Erbenheim in Germany, where they were parked on the race course without an opportunity for repairs.

The three vehicles of *Abt. 13* were less fortunate; two caught fire, and the third was set ablaze by its crew after gear trouble rendered it immobile. The Iwuy-Rieux counterattack marked the swansong of the German armored force.

The last German tank action of the war occurred on 1 November 1918, when *Sturm Pz. Abt. 12, 13,* and *14* were deployed to support a counterattack by the *28th Inf. Div.* near Sebourg and Valenciennes. *Sturm Pz. Abt. 12* and *13* fielded only five *Mark IV* tanks, of which only three made it past the start line. Both *Sturm Pz. Abt. 12* tanks were disabled by British artillery and the sole *Sturm Pz. Abt. 13* tank lagged so far behind the assault troops that it never saw combat action. The detachments and their surviving tanks were released on the evening of 1 November, and on the following day, they prepared for their march back. The railway journey led them straight into Germany, and on 8 November they were detrained at Erbenheim near Wiesbaden.

On 9 November 1918 all Imperial tank detachments were disbanded, and transportable combat vehicles were integrated into the 1st Reichswehr Group (*Reichswehr Gruppenkommando 1*) at the Berlin-Lankwitz barracks. The combat vehicles, found in an unsuitable state for transport, remained in Erbenheim. In mid-December 1918 French units discovered them, encountering some burned-out vehicles while others were dismantled and scrapped.

Beutepanzer in action
On 1 June 1918 *Sturm Pz. Abt. 1, 13, 14,* supported by the 238th Inf. Div, launched an attack northwest of Fort de la Pompelle, west of Rheims. The tank attack did not go well. Two tanks broke down before reaching the start line, and a third one had to retreat to German lines due to mechanical problems. Two others were lost in action.
The only tank from *Sturm Pz. Abt. 12,* attached to *Abt. 13,* lost during the operation against Fort de la Pompelle. Note the red rings (cockade) marking and an individual tactical number (5). (AC)

Tanks from *Sturm Pz. Abt. 13* on a refueling stop photographed before the (Third) Battle of the Aisne, which took place near Rheims, France, on 31 May 1918. (IWM)

A *Mark IV* 'Female' tank was destroyed by a mine and French artillery north of Perthes, France, on 2 October 1918. The tank is from *Sturm Pz. Abt. 11* which can be recognized by a white ring (cockade) marking and an individual tactical number (4). (AC)

4
Uniforms, Personal Equipment and Weapons

Pre-war (parade) uniforms

All branches of *Verkehrstruppen*, including railway troops, motor troops, signal troops, air shipment troops and flight service troops, prior to 1914 wore a dark blue (*Dunkelblau*) parade dress (*Waffenrock)* with a black collar, black Swedish cuffs, and silver buttons. Most, but not all, units wore double ornamental braid (*Garde Litzen*) on the collar, in white for enlisted ranks and silver for commissioned officers. The straps were light gray with red cyphers/letters, except for Bavaria, which wore red straps with yellow cyphers until May 1914, when the light gray straps were adopted. The collar, cuffs, and piping on the front opening and rear skirt was scarlet. This color served to identify the branch of service according to the *Waffenfarbe* system, where *Waffen* refered to 'arm of service' and *Farbe* denotes 'color.' The incorporation of colors for identification purposes into German military uniforms dated back to 1870, with the Prussians adopting piped shoulder straps as early as 1835. However, these earlier colors cannot strictly be considered *Waffenfarbe* as they did not signify specific arms of service but had somewhat various classifications. It was not until 15 September 1915 that the concept of *Waffenfarbe*, in its recognized sense, was formally introduced. New dress regulations were established across the Imperial Army, defining specific basic colors for each arm. It is worth noting that the Imperial authorities of the time were aware of the historical associations between specific colors and particular formations, and they acknowledged this by incorporating these colors into the newly introduced *Waffenfarben*.

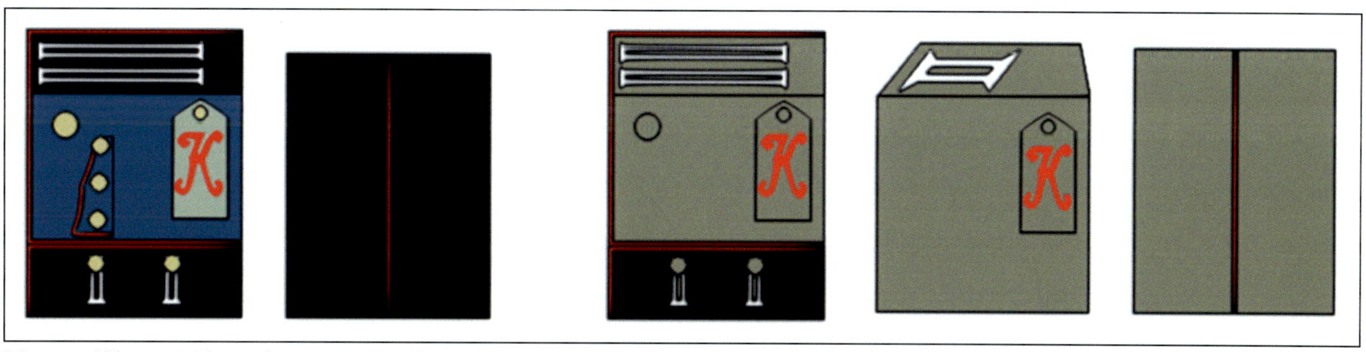

Motorized Transport Troops (*Kraftfahrtruppen*) wore a parade uniform consisting of a dark blue jacket paired with black trousers while their field uniform was entirely field gray. ##

Straps and emblems

Commissioned officers of the *Kraftfahrtruppen* had silver cord shoulder straps with a gold cypher 'K'. At the same time, enlisted ranks sported a red embroidered 'K' on an unpiped field gray strap, sometimes with red unit numbers from previous assignments below the 'K'. Special emblems denoting car drivers and motorcyclists, depicting a car or motorcycle, were introduced for collar patches. These emblems, typically made of bronze pressings, were designed and produced but were not widely worn due to limited manufacturing quantities.

The *Kraftfahrtruppen* (Motorized Transport Troops) uniform specific elements (1914)

<table>
<tr><th>Unit and Garrison</th><th>Straps</th><th>Coat of arms (Wappen)</th></tr>
<tr><td>(Kraftfahr Bn.) Motor Transport Battalions</td><td></td><td></td></tr>
<tr><td>Kraftfahr-Bataillon
(Berlin) Garde-Korps</td><td>Light Gray
w/ Scarlet K</td><td>Silver Guard Eagle on Pickelhaube (1)</td></tr>
<tr><td colspan="3">Wappen note: 2nd Coy / Sachsen (Saxon) Section - Pickelhaube gilt Wappen on silver star, 3rd Coy / Württemberg Section - Pickelhaube gilt Württemberg Wappen in silver with Guard Star identical to Dragoner Regt Nr. 26.</td></tr>
<tr><td>Bayer. Luft- u. Kraftfahrer-Bataillon
(München) I Bayerisches Armee Korps</td><td>Red
w/ Yellow L</td><td>Silver Bavarian Wappen on Tschako</td></tr>
<tr><td>(VPK) Commission for Transport Technology</td><td></td><td></td></tr>
<tr><td>Verkehrstechnische
Prüfungskommission Abteilung (Berlin) Garde-Korps</td><td>Light Gray
w/ Scarlet V</td><td>Silver Guard Eagle on Pickelhaube</td></tr>
</table>

Field uniform

The *AKO* (*Allgemeine Königliche Order*) from 19 April 1907 announced the release of the new German uniform, known as the M.1907 *Feldrock*, made of a heavy wool green-gray (*Feldgrau*) material retaining the various state and regimental distinctions. The new uniform was piped in *Waffenfarbe* colors, with colored piping sewn around the bottom edge of the collar, on the front fly, on the cuffs and flaps, and the rear skirt formation. Shoulder straps were a slip-on pattern and piped in Army Corps colors or unit-facing colors, depending on the unit/branch of service. The upper part of the cloth lining above the waist was white, and the lower part, including the rear skirts, was gray. In the waist were fitted ties to allow the wearer to adjust the waist for proper fit. Two large removable hooks in the shape of buttons are attached above the rear skirt formation and were used to carry the extra weight of the belt and its attached equipment. On the hips, two tombac side hooks were sewn to help distribute the weight. The *Feldrock* was intended for field use only, and the old *Dunkelblau* uniforms were maintained for all other occasions. Additionally, these troops wore straight, baggy trousers and puttees, all in field gray. The *Feldrock* had to be simplified in 1915, replacing the elaborate Brandenburg and Swedish cuffs with simpler turned-back cuffs.

Uniforms
Motorized transport troops in pre-war uniforms (dark blue tunic and field gray trousers). The collar patches were dark blue and piped in red, and topped with a small metal car badge. (AC)

Soldiers of the Royal Bavarian Air- and Motortransport Battalion (*Kgl. Bayer. Luft- u. Kraftfahrer-Bataillon*). Note the soldier armed with the *Kar98* rifle. He wears a pre-war dark blue tunic with guard lace on collar and Swedish cuffs., and leather *Tschako* with (silver) Bavarian *Wappen* and blue/white *Feldzeichen*. The shoulder straps were red with a yellow script 'L'. (AC)

Soldiers of the Royal Prussian Motorized Transport Bn (*Kraftfahr Bnn. 1 Komp. Garde Reserve*) 1909. Soldiers on the left wear re-war dark blue tunic with guard lace on collar and Swedish cuffs, and the *Pickelhaube* with (silver) Guard Eagle. The two men on the right wear full-leather driver uniforms. Note: *Reserve 1909, 280 Tage* (days) denoted soldiers who had fulfilled their active duty commitment and entered the ranks of the reserves. (AC)

Uniforms
Motor troops hailing from a reserve unit stationed in Prussian territory, identifiable by the homeland registration number plates (MK) on their vehicles, along with their parade uniforms featuring Swedish cuffs and visored caps. Only a solitary soldier dons the customary leather jacket indicative of a driver. (AC)

A gathering of drivers adorned in complete leather attire. Observe the rubber tires, exclusive to the early years of the Great War, gradually supplanted by solid metal wheels. (AC)

Personnel from the transport column of the *221.Inf.Div.* The photograph was likely taken in a motor park/depot, as evidenced by some soldiers or mechanics attired in fatigued dresses. (AC)

Headdress

During the early stages of the war, all transport troops, except railway units, wore the *Tschako* with brass fittings for standard duties, while railway units wore the *Pickelhaube* with brass fittings. Over time, the primary headgear for the transport troops evolved into the field cap (*mütze*), which had a blackened leather visor and chinstrap, with scarlet piping at the top and bottom, along with a scarlet welt. The chinstrap had black metal or gray-painted buttons, with some variations in materials such as copper, zinc, or nickel. From late 1915 to early 1916, peaks and chinstraps were issued in gray. In October 1918 it was decided to discontinue the M.1908 cap, removing the visor and chinstrap.

The standard field headdress for the Motorized Transport Troops was the steel trench helmet, which provided protection to soldiers engaged close to combat areas or on sentinel duties.

Black leather suit

Members of the *Kraftfahrtruppen*, especially drivers and tank crew members, were issued leather uniforms (*Lederanzug für Kraftfahrer* M.1907) to shield them from the elements while driving the often open vehicles of the era. These leather jackets (*Lederlitewka*) displayed several variations, particularly in the collar, collar insignia, and button types. Early photographs typically show jackets with white metal automobile emblems on a dark blue collar, fastened with nickel or new silver buttons attached to a leather strip. Later versions often lacked patches, featuring a blackened leather collar and either metal or larger, darker buttons, possibly made of bone. The drivers also donned trousers crafted from chrome-tanned black calfskin leather, lined with dark gray wool flannel, and tailored similarly to service dress trousers. Early versions retained red piping along each outer side of the leg, but this feature was less common in later iterations. Leather gaiters were worn with the trousers, typically in blackened leather with a strap and buckle at the top and a hook attachment at the bottom to secure around the leg. However, these gaiters became less prevalent toward the end of the war due to leather supply shortages. Additionally, drivers wore leather caps (*Ledermütze*) made of black chrome-tanned leather featuring red leather piping and two cockades. Complementing the uniform were goggles designed to protect drivers from wind, dust, and debris while operating vehicles, similar to those worn by aviation personnel.

Work overalls

For dirty work around the vehicles mechanics typically wore simple black two-piece denim overalls. Drivers occasionally wore one-piece suits in gray, sometimes made of heavy cloth or leather. These suits were paired with a heavy belt featuring a frame buckle and metal eyelets, along with a low padded crash helmet painted field gray. Shoulder loops and uniform buttons were attached to the overalls, suggesting that shoulder straps from the service dress were occasionally worn with them.

Uniforms
Motorized Transport Troops, in leather jackets called *Lederlitewka.* Jackets came with and without the automobile collar emblem, the difference being that the ones with the device indicated that the wearer had earned his military driver's license (*Führerschein*). (AC)

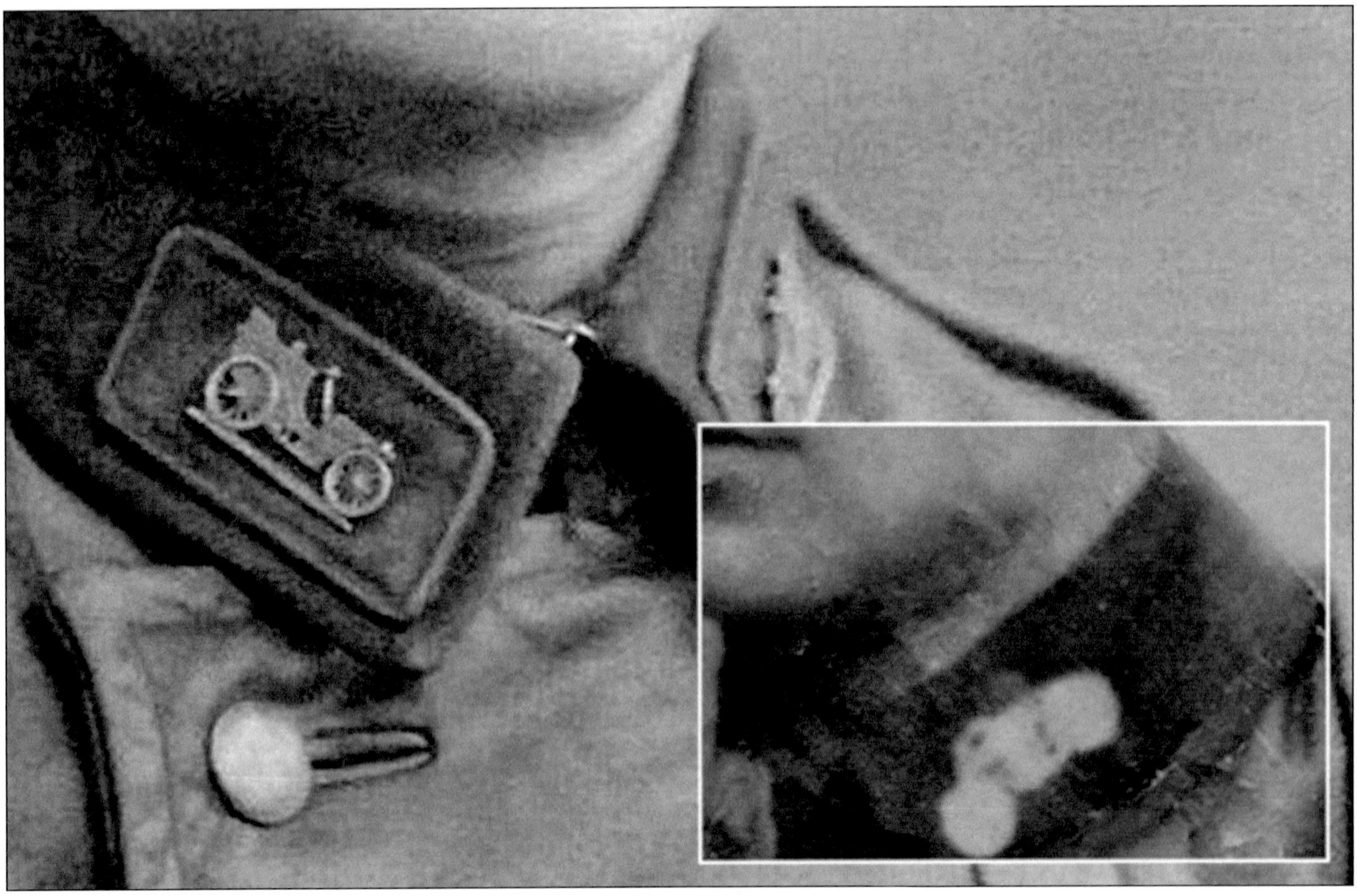

The collar emblems signifying car drivers and motorcyclists were made out of bronze pressings. (AC)

Straps with a brass 'K' (for *Kraftfahrtruppen*) were introduced in 1911. In the spring of 1916, the brass was replaced by a red chain stitched letter 'K'. (AC)

Motorized transport troops versus combat troops

While on duty, truck drivers wore full leather protective gear to shield themselves from the cold and wind in half-open cabins. On the other hand, tank crews preferred to wear lighter blouses, which were more suited to the hot and smoky environment inside the tank compartments. (AC)

Two crew members of an *A7V* from *Sturm Pz. Abt.1*. The one on the left wears a gray-painted crash helmet made of blocked leather with a padded rim, a blouse of which the collar *Litzen* are just visible, and a one-piece gray suit of either leather or heavy cloth. The man on the right wears a British facemask and certainly wears a suit of fabric rather than leather. Chainmail masks were used to protect crew members from rivets and flying pieces of metal that got knocked off inside the tank. (AC)

Members of the *Mark IV* of the *Sturm Pz. Abt.14* (Heinz). The man in the center has a gray-painted crash helmet (*Sturzhelm / Sturzkappe*), to protect his heads from the risk of injury within the cramped and often turbulent confines of the tank, and a one-piece green-gray suit of heavy cloth. Note that the rest of the crew wore steel trench helmets that would be green-gray in color. (AC)

Armored fighting vehicle crew dress

The troops serving in armored car and tank detachments were recruited from various branches of the military according to their specialties: artillery gunners, signalers from communication units, drivers and mechanics from transportation motor units, and machine gunners from the infantry. Commanding officers were primarily from the *Kraftfahrtruppen*.

It is interesting to note that the crews of combat motor detachments retained the distinctions of their original branch of service uniforms. Signalers and artillery personnel were identified by black bands and red piping on their uniforms, while machine gunners usually sported red bands and piping. Signalers' shoulder straps would bear 'T' instead of 'K', while artillerymen would have red straps with a yellow 'bomb above yellow unit numbers' for Field Regiments, and yellow straps with red numbers below red crossed cannon for Foot Artillery Regiments. Machine gunners typically wore field gray straps with red or white piping and red numbers or white piping with a common number like '13'. Gunners from Machine-Gun Sharpshooter Detachments might wear a gray oval patch on the upper left arm with a red stylized machine gun.

Tank crews in combat areas often wore black leather or work suits, with non-standard clothing being common. Some crew members wore transitional jackets resembling a mix of the old 1910 field tunic and the blouse. These jackets might feature piping in branch colours around the collar, front closure and/or cuffs, pockets where they shouldn't be, or exposed buttons down the front.

All ranks wore two cockades on their caps: the black/white/red Reichs cockade on the crown and the state cockade on the band. For most personnel, the state cockade would be black/white/black for Prussia, but the Bavarian 13rd Assault Tank Detachment (*Sturm Pz. Abt. 13*) wore light blue/white/light blue.

The peaked cap could be worn with or without a black chinstrap, with no apparent significance to the variation.

Tank crew members sometimes wore chainmail face-masks, which added additional protection (against shrapnel) to the face while inside the tank.

Personal weapons and equipment

Personal equipment of armored cars and tank detachments was limited to a belt, holsters for either the *Luger* P08 automatic or the M.79 revolver, fighting daggers, driving goggles, and gas mask canisters.

The regular *Kraftfahrtruppen* were equipped with rifles, particularly the *Gewehr* 98, however, these firearms were primarily utilized for guard duties, given that transport troops were seldom involved in combat missions.

Original belts were made of natural brown leather, with brass buckles featuring a nickel silver inlay. From 1915, leather equipment included blackened buckles painted over in gray or manufactured in steel with a gray finish.

Uniforms
German motorcyclists in leather clothing and distinctive leather helmets. Off-duty motorcycle drivers commonly wore field peak caps. (AC)

During the Great War, the majority of German drivers wore goggles for protection. The lenses were replaceable. While off-duty, googles were kept in a special case attached to the belt. In staff cars, NCOs typically occupied the front seats, while officers were seated in the back. (AC)

A photograph taken in the French town of La Bassée in October 1914 depicts a German driver from the *VI.Armee*, amidst the so-called 'Race to the Sea' aimed at encircling the northern flank of Franco-British Forces. The driver is wearing a helmet and carrying a gas mask canister, items that were scarcely utilized by transport personnel at the onset of trench warfare (AC).

Afterword

At the outbreak of First World War, the ability to field and maintain massive armies was essential for all the major powers involved. As nations mobilized for total war, the scale of military operations grew to unprecedented levels. The railways quickly became an indispensable asset in this effort, providing a crucial logistical backbone that enabled the rapid movement of vast numbers of troops, artillery, ammunition, and other supplies directly to the front lines. This extensive railway network allowed armies to sustain continuous operations over extended periods, something that was vital in the context of modern industrial warfare.

While the railways were effective in delivering men and material to the vicinity of the front lines, the real logistical challenges began approximately 10 kilometers behind the front. This zone was critical but difficult to manage due to the fragmented and chaotic nature of the battlefield environment. The terrain in this area was typically crisscrossed with trenches, shell craters, and barbed wire, making it challenging to transport supplies using traditional methods.

Initially, this crucial gap between the railheads and the front lines was covered by a combination of light trains, which could navigate narrower gauge tracks laid closer to the front, and horse-drawn wagons, which had been the mainstay of military logistics for centuries. However, as the war progressed, the limitations of these methods became increasingly apparent. The slow pace of horse-drawn wagons and the vulnerability of both horses and light trains to enemy artillery and machine-gun fire highlighted the need for more efficient and robust transport solutions.

In response to these challenges, motor vehicles began to be introduced in greater numbers. Trucks and other motorized transport vehicles provided a faster and more reliable means of moving supplies, ammunition, and even troops closer to the front lines. The introduction of motor vehicles marked a significant shift in military logistics, as they could operate over rough terrain that was impassable to trains and allowed for greater flexibility in responding to the rapidly changing conditions of the battlefield.

Unfortunately for the Germans their industrial base, which was extensive but not centralized, could hardly scale up production. Numerous small and medium-sized manufacturers existed, each with its own designs, production methods, and capabilities. This fragmentation led to a lack of standardization, making it challenging to produce vehicles in large quantities and to ensure that parts were interchangeable between different models. The result was a logistical nightmare, as maintenance and repairs became increasingly difficult, with many units in the field lacking the necessary spare parts for their specific vehicles.

Compounding this problem was Germany's lack of access to vital strategic resources. The Allied naval blockade effectively cut off Germany from global trade routes, severely limiting the importation of essential materials like oil and rubber. As the war dragged on, the scarcity of these materials became more acute, forcing the Germans to resort to inferior substitutes that were less effective and more difficult to produce.

Static trench warfare also profoundly influenced the development of motorized combat vehicles. In an effort to break the stalemate on the Western Front and restore battlefield mobility, Western designers, engineers, and entrepreneurs developed various technological innovations. These innovations led to the invention of motorized armored fighting vehicles, which played a crucial role in helping the Allies win the Great War. The Germans, however, were unable to adequately respond to this emerging threat. They were both unwilling and unable to create a substantial motorized armored force and the necessary supporting infrastructure.

One of the primary reasons for Germany's limited progress in developing armored fighting vehicles during the First World War was the deep-seated skepticism within the Imperial General Staff regarding their effectiveness on the battlefield. Despite the revolutionary potential that tanks and other armored vehicles represented, many high-ranking military leaders in the German command viewed them with considerable doubt. This skepticism stemmed from several factors, including the perceived vulnerability of these vehicles to artillery fire, anti-tank obstacles, and infantry attacks. The General Staff believed that the slow speed and mechanical unreliability of early tanks made them easy targets that could not significantly alter the dynamics of entrenched warfare. This entrenched belief persisted despite the increasingly clear evidence from the Western Front, where the Allies, particularly the British and French, were beginning to demonstrate the potential of tanks to break through enemy lines and restore mobility to the battlefield.

The few German combat motorized units that were created were modest in scope and deployed in insufficient numbers to have a meaningful impact on the war.

Although the Germans were ultimately defeated the experiences and lessons they gained during the conflict were crucial in shaping the future of their military strategy, technology, and organization. The harsh realities and challenges faced on the battlefields

The Swan Song
Despite facing overwhelming odds, the German tank troops, continued to strive for expansion and operational effectiveness until the very last weeks of the Great War. The last two detachments equipped with *Mark IV* tanks (*Sturm Pz. Abt. 15 and 16*) underwent intensive training at the *BAKP 20* raining ground in Charleroi, and on 27 September they were assigned to Army Group *Kronprinz*, which promptly reassigned them to the XVII Army Corps. (AC)

A *Mark IV* during exercises in the autumn of 1918 before entering combat. (AC)

of the First World War, particularly in the realm of mechanized warfare, served as a profound and invaluable education for the German military, influencing their future approach to warfare in the years to come.

The Germans, despite their initial shortcomings in motorized transport and the development of armored vehicles, came to understand the transformative potential of these technologies. The logistical difficulties, such as the lack of standardized vehicles, inadequate motorization of supply lines, and the challenges of maintaining mechanized units, highlighted the importance of a well-coordinated and resource-efficient military machine. These lessons would later lead to the meticulous planning and development of more reliable and standardized military vehicles in the interwar period.

The Great War highlighted to visionaries like Lutz and Guderian the critical need for rapid and flexible movement of troops and equipment supported by armoured fighting vehicles, which ultimately led to the development of the *Blitzkrieg* doctrine. This doctrine, which emphasized speed, surprise, and maneuver over static trench warfare, began to take shape already within the *Reichswehr* and was later perfected by the *Wehrmacht*.

The technological innovations during the First World War, although not always fully realized during the conflict, laid the groundwork for future advancements. The experience with early tanks, though limited, demonstrated the potential of armored warfare. German engineers and military planners took these early experiences and invested heavily in research and development during the interwar period, leading to significant advancements in tank design, aircraft, and other military technologies.

In essence, while the defeat in First World War was a significant blow to Germany, the conflict served as a crucible in which the foundations of modern German military doctrine were forged. The experiences gained, though born out of hardship and loss, provided the German military with the insights and impetus needed to develop the strategies, technologies, and organizational reforms that would later define their approach to warfare in Second World War.

Beutepanzer in action

Throughout October and November 1918 the German army continued to use tanks on the Western Front. However, despite their efforts, the German offensives ultimately proved unsuccessful, and the war ended on 11 November 1918 with an Allied victory.

A German tank near Le Quesnoy, capture by the Canterbury Regiment. Two New Zealand soldiers are inspecting it. This photograph was taken in early October 1918. (NLNZealand)

A picture showing *Mark IV* on a rail platform in September / October 1918. (Photo: Musée des Deux Guerres Mondiales / BDIC)

An *A7V* (503) and *Mark IV*, both in a semi-dismantled state, probably at Charleroi after their capture by the British in November 1918. Note the late-war *Balkenkreuz* markings with a white background. (AC)

Appendix I
Technical specifications of selected fighting vehicles

Daimler M.1915 Armored Car	
Weight	9,800kg.
Length	5.6m.
Height	3.85m.
Width	2.1m.
Armor	6-9 mm.
Engine	4-cylinder Daimler petrol, 80 hp
Main armament	Three 7.92mm MG 08/15 machine-guns.
Crew	10
Performance	Maximum speed 38kph. Road range of 250km.
Production	1 piece

Büssing A5P Armored Car	
Weight	13,300kg.
Length	9.5m.
Height	3.5m.
Width	2.1m.
Armor	6-9 mm.
Engine	6-cylinder Büssing «Otto» petrol, 90 hp (67.14 kW)
Main armament	Three 7.92mm MG 08/15 machine-guns.
Crew	10
Performance	Maximum speed 34km/h. Road range of 240km.
Production	1 piece

Ehrhardt M.1917 EV4 Armored Car	
Weight	7,500kg.
Length	5.3m.
Height	2,85m.
Width	2.0m.
Armor	6-9 mm.
Engine	6-cylinder Daimler petrol, 80 hp
Main armament	Three 7.92mm MG 08/15 machine-guns.
Crew	6 to 9
Performance	Maximum speed 61km/h. Road range of 250km.
Production	12 pieces

A7V Tank	
Weight	32,510kg.
Length	7.35–8.00m.
Height	3.40–3.50m.
Width	3.10–3.20m.
Armour	Front 30mm; sides 20mm; roof 10mm; other 20mm.
Fuel tank capacity	500 litres of petrol (two 250 litre tanks).
Engine	Two Daimler 165204 four-cylinder petrol power units, centrally mounted, each producing 75kW (100hp). This provided a power-to-weight ratio of 5.1 kW/ton (6.8hp/ton).
Main armament:	One 5.7cm Maxim-Nordenfelt or Sokol cannon.
Secondary armament:	Six 7.92mm MG 08/15 machine-guns.
Ammunition:	5.7cm – 90 canister rounds, 54 anti-tank rounds, 36 HE rounds. These 180 rounds represented the mandated scales, but a total of up to 500 rounds of 5.7cm cannon ammunition were carried in practice. 7.92mm – up to 60 belts, each of 250 rounds, was the laid down scale. However, up to 36,000 rounds of machine-gun ammunition were usually carried in combat.
Performance	Maximum speed – 9–15km/h (roads) and 4–8km/h (cross-country), with a ditch crossing capability of 2.1m and ground clearance of 19 to 40cm (which limited its movement across trenches and on excessively soft or muddy ground). Range on roads – 60–80km and 30–35km cross-country.
Production	20 pieces (A7V *Geländewagen*, 53, (A7V *Flakpanzer*, 3)

A7V/U Tank	
Weight	39,600kg.
Length	8.38–8.50m.
Height	3.14m.
Width	4.69m.
Armor	Front 30mm; sides 20mm; roof 20mm; other 20mm
Fuel tank capacity	500 liters of petrol (two 250 liter tanks).
Engine	Two Daimler 165204 four-cylinder petrol power units, centrally mounted, each producing 75kW (100 horsepower). This provided a power-to- weight ratio of 5.1 kW/ton (6.8hp/ton).
Main armament	Two 5.7cm Maxim-Nordenfelt or Sokol cannon, or two 7.7cm cannon
Secondary armament	Four to six 7.92mm MG 08/15 machine-guns.
Performance	Maximum speed 12km/h roads) and about 5km/h (cross-country).
Production	1 piece

K-Wagen Tank	
Weight	150,370 to 152,400kg.
Length	12.7m.
Height	3.0m.
Width	3.0m (6.0m including side sponsons).
Armor	10–30mm.
Engine	Two V6 Daimler-Benz aero power units, each producing 485 kW(650 hp), with an electro-magnetic clutch transmission system.
Main armament	Four 7.7cm cannon.
Secondary armament	Seven 7.92mm MG 08/15 machine-guns.
Flamethrowers	An option to fit flamethrowers was considered but not adopted.
Ammunition	800 rounds of 7.7cm cannon ammunition and 21,000 rounds of 7.92mm machine-gun ammunition.
Performance	Maximum speed 7.5km/h.

Appendix II

Development Timeline of Selected German Motorized Vehicles (1914-1918)

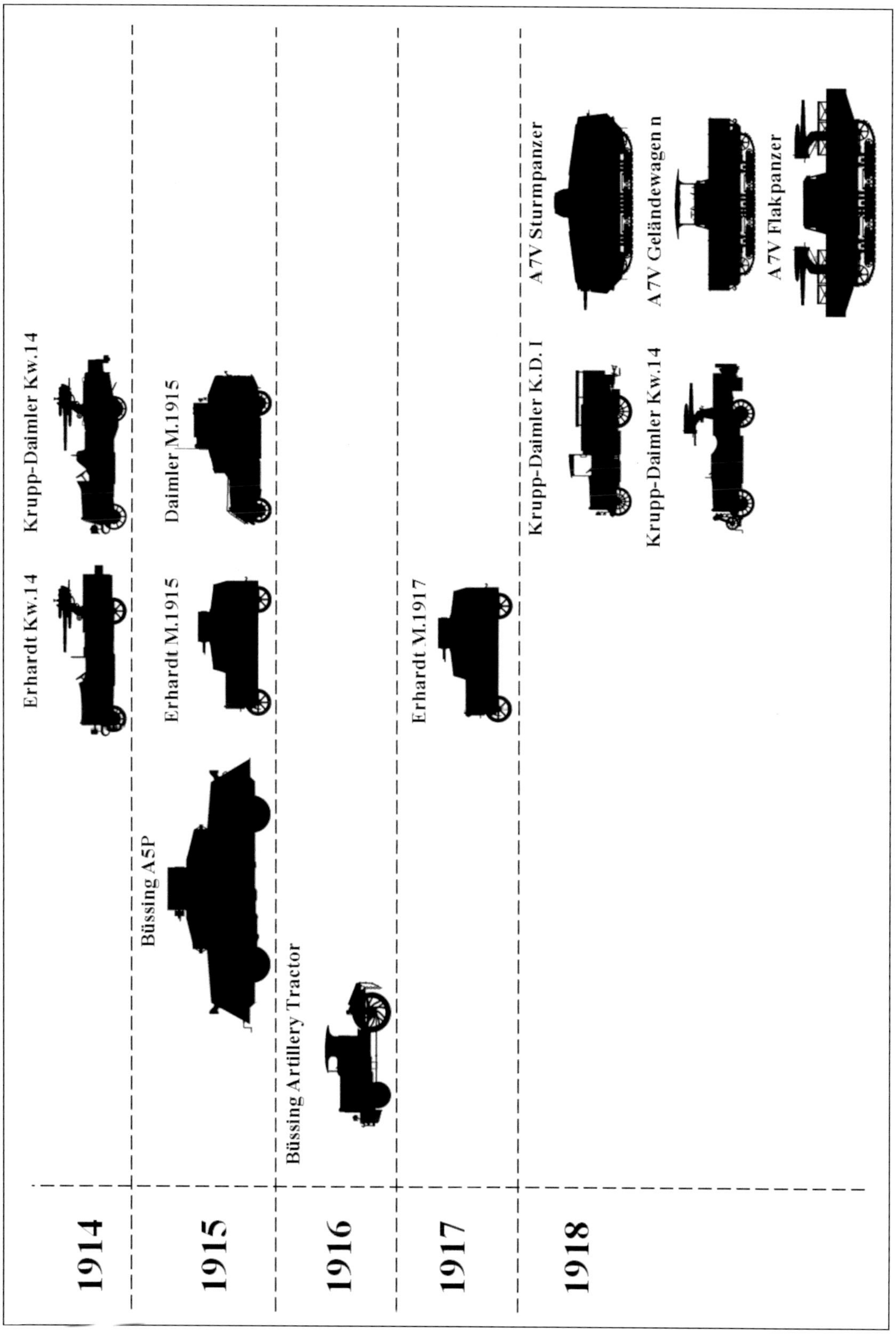

Bibliography

Printed books

Johannes Denecke, *Tarnanstriche des deutschen Heeres 1914 bis heute* (Bernard & Graefe, 2001)
D.S.V. Fosten & R.J. Marrion, *The German Army 1914-18,* Osprey MAA80 (Osprey Publishing, 1978)
Andreas Herzfeld, *Militärische Abkürzungen an Kraftfahrzeugen im 1. Weltkrieg: Ein Wörterbuch* (Flaggenkunde, 2019)
Max Hundleby & Rainer Strasheim, *Sturmpanzer: The German A7V Tank and the Captured British Mark IV Tanks of World War* (G T Foulis & Co Ltd, 1990)
Herbert Jager, *German Artillery of World War One* (Crowood Press, 2001)
Stanislav Kirilec, *Avtomobili-zenitki Pervoi mirovoi voiny* (Jauza, 2021)
Fred Koch, *Beutepanzer im Ersten Weltkrieg* (Podzung Pallas, 1994)
Jürgen Kraus, *Handbuch der Verbände und Truppen des deutschen Heeres 1914–1918, Kraftfahrtruppen Vols. 1 & 2* (Verlag Militaria, 2023)
Thomas Müller, *Die Bayerische Sturm-Panzer-Kraftwagen-Abteilung 13* (Verlag Veit Scherzer, 2013)
Klaus Paprotka, *Taktische Einsätze der Sturmpanzerwagen A7V im Jahre 1918* (Bernard & Graefe Verlag, 2003)
Wolfgang Schneider & Reiner Strasheim, *German Tanks in World War I. The A7V and Early Tank Development* (Schiffer Publishing, 1990)
Rainer Strasheim, *Beute-Tanks - British Tanks in German Service Vol. 1/2, Tankograd WWI Nr 1003/4* (Tankograd Publishing, 2011)
Rainer Strasheim, *Panzer-Kraftwagen - Armoured Cars of the German Army and Freikorps, Tankograd WWI Nr 1007* (Tankograd Publishing, 2013)
Rainer Strasheim & Max Hundleby, *Sturmpanzer, A7V - First of the Panzers, Tankograd WWI Nr 1001* (Tankograd Publishing, 2020)
Nigel Thomas, *The German Army in WWI 1914-15 (I)* MAA394; *1915-17 (II)*, Osprey MAA 407; *1917-18 (III),* MAA 419 (Osprey Publishing, 2003-2004)
Carlos de Diego Vaquerizo & Ricardo Recio Cardon , *Deutsche Panzer 1917-1918* (Abteilung 502, 2022)
Carlos de Diego Vaquerizo, *Panzerwaffe Tarnfarben. Camouflage Colours and Organization of the German Armed Forces (1917-1945)* (Abteilung 502, 2021)
Jochen Vollert, *Lastkraftwagen - German Military Trucks Vol. 2, Tankograd WWI Nr 1011* (Tankograd Publishing, 2021)
Jochen Vollert, *Spezialfahrzeuge - German Specialised Motor Vehicles, Tankograd WWI Nr 1012* (Tankograd Publishing, 2022)
Steven J. Zaloga, *German Panzers 1914-1918,* Osprey NV127 (Osprey Publishing, 2006)

Journal articles

Krzysztof Fudalej, 'Cesarska armia niemiecka i motoryzacja podczas Wielkiej Wojny', *Technika Wojskowa Historia 1/2021*, pp. 66-72
Krzysztof Fudalej, 'Skromne początki. Czołgi, obrona przeciwpancerna i armia niemiecka podczas I w.ś.', *Przegląd Historyczno-Wojskowy 2020/1,* pp. 62-100.

Archival Sources

Bundesarchiv - Abteilung Militärarchiv (BArch-MA), N 610/15, N 610/16, N 610/19

Websites

https://www.feldgrau-forum.com/
https://www.flickr.com/photos/drakegoodman/
https://archiv-axel-oskar-mathieu.de/